WHAT PEOPLE ARE SAYING ABOUT *HOW DO I RETIRE?*

"Richard Baker has laid out a practical process for transitioning into retirement. He has a God-given ability to offer sound advice in easily understandable instructions, and his heartfelt concern for people is evident on every page. This book is a result of years of experience guiding people through the retirement process, making it required reading for everyone within a few years of retirement!"

STEVE GREEN
PRESIDENT, HOBBY LOBBY STORES, INC.
CHAIRMAN OF THE BOARD, MUSEUM OF THE BIBLE

"Richard Baker has written a must-read book for anyone seriously considering retirement and wanting to feel comfortable and financially ready for this major life decision. The book is relatable in so many ways and takes the overwhelming topic of retirement and breaks it down into manageable chunks of information. Thinking about different stages of retirement (early, middle, and late) was especially insightful. This approach made me reevaluate my retirement planning. Completing the monthly expense analysis was extremely eye-opening, too. I am now more relaxed and better prepared for my retirement."

TRAVIS MCNAIL VICE PRESIDENT, HUMAN
RESOURCES, DOLLAR TREE STORES

"A timely resource. Richard Baker has woven complex concepts into a clarifying book to give guidance to those preparing for and participating in retirement. His most classic line is, 'Remember, retirement is not a finish line but a starting line to a new season of life.' Insightful treasures in every chapter — a must read."

JOHN YEATS EXECUTIVE DIRECTOR-TREASURER,
MISSOURI BAPTIST CONVENTION RECORDING
SECRETARY, SOUTHERN BAPTIST CONVENTION

"In *How Do I Retire?*, Richard Baker provides a guide for those eager to learn key aspects of retirement and be proactive in planning. With the care of a trusted friend or family member, Richard unpacks financial concepts in simple terms with practical examples. This is a resource you'll dog-ear and reference again and again."

> ERIN B. DAVIS BUSINESS CONSULTANT AT ERIN B. DAVIS, LLC FORMER CHIEF OPERATING OFFICER, HONEYWELL OPERATING SYSTEM

"Richard Baker has written an outstanding and practical retirement guide in *How Do I Retire?* His knowledge and experience in financial planning offer the reader a useful and helpful roadmap to navigating retirement."

> SAM F. HAMRA FOUNDER & CHAIRMAN, HAMRA ENTERPRISES, WHICH OWNS AND OPERATES 170 RESTAURANTS WITH MORE THAN 7,000 EMPLOYEES

"As a huge proponent of financial literacy, I appreciate Dr. Baker's passion for helping people prepare for and execute a happy and purposeful retirement. I encourage anyone who has those goals — and that should be everyone! — to avail themselves of this practical and accessible wisdom."

> TIM GARRISON FORMER UNITED STATES ATTORNEY AT THE JUSTICE DEPARTMENT

HOW DO I RETIRE?
A PRACTICAL GUIDE TO BECOMING FINANCIALLY READY FOR RETIREMENT

RICHARD L. BAKER

Copyright © 2022 by Richard L. Baker

All rights reserved. No part of this book may be reproduced, stored in a retrieval system, or transmitted in any form or by any means, except for brief quotations in critical reviews or articles, without prior written permission from the author.

Unless otherwise indicated, Scripture quotations are from the Holman Christian Standard Bible (HCSB).

Paperback ISBN: 978-1-7372785-6-6

Hardcover ISBN: 978-1-7373785-7-3

eBook ISBN: 978-1-7372785-8-0

HSP Production Team

Executive editor: John Yeats
Editor: Rob Phillips
Cover design: Laura Schembre
Interior graphics: Tony Boes
Layout: Brianna Boes
Production management: Gary Ledbetter
Electronic production: Brianna Boes
Proofreading: Christie Dowell, Nancy Phillips

High Street Press is the publishing arm of the Missouri Baptist Convention (MBC) and exists because of the generous support of Missouri Baptists through the Cooperative Program. To learn more about the MBC and the way 1,800 affiliated churches cooperate voluntarily for the sake of the gospel, visit mobaptist.org. To learn more about High Street Press, visit highstreet.press.

CONTENTS

Foreword	ix
Introduction	xi
Chapter One *A Starting Point*	1
Chapter Two *Your Monthly Spending Plan*	11
Chapter Three *Getting the Most Out of Social Security*	27
Chapter Four *Income*	41
Chapter Five *Investment Tools*	57
Chapter Six *Estate Planning*	73
Chapter Seven *Financial Plan*	87
Chapter Eight *Where Do I Go from Here?*	97
Additional Resources	103
Key Definitions	105
The Ultimate Retirement	109
Endnotes	113
About the Author	117

To my beautiful brown-eyed wife, Sara: You are a blessing to me in so many ways. Thank you for the many hours you have spent on this book. Thank you for cleaning up my grammar and for always thinking about the reader's perspective.

To my Anna Grace: You continually amaze me. I won't be surprised by the great success you're going to have in college and your career. Your potential is unlimited.

To my Micah: I have an earned doctorate and am a gifted strategist, but you, as a freshman in high school, frequently beat me in chess. I'm excited to see how the Lord uses that mind of yours.

To High Street Press: Thank you for believing in me and helping me help others.

To my clients: Thank you for the privilege of serving you and your families.

FOREWORD

I am honored to preview this book. I am a recent retiree as president of Bass Pro Shops and Cabela's, so the issues and considerations are fresh for me. Certainly, after decades of working, saving, and accumulating assets, the game changes – in retirement the script is flipped as you begin to pay yourself from the portfolio of assets you have generated over time. There are many things to consider, both financially and emotionally. One of the most difficult parts about preparing for retirement is thinking about life after work. Retirement is a life-changing decision, and a financial professional can be an invaluable resource to help navigate a real milestone in life's journey.

This book provides an easily available template developed by an accomplished wealth advisor. Since becoming a financial professional in 1996, Dr. Richard Baker has developed a diverse background and expertise to assist clients in retirement planning, business succession, and charitable giving. He has implemented strategies to build family wealth and protect those assets over time.

Dr. Baker earned a B. S. in business from College of the Ozarks (affectionately known as Hard Work U), a master's degree (Divinity), and a doctorate (Leadership) from Midwestern Baptist Theological Seminary. Dr. Baker is the ideal advisor, in my opinion, to help families build and protect wealth. Dr. Baker has lived the American dream, working his way through his entire educational journey, building his business, and creating wealth over the entirety of his career. He has demonstrated the kind of discipline, persistence, and patience that it takes to build sustainability in a financial plan. Wealth can only be achieved by accumulating assets; increasing income alone does not build assets.

To develop a meaningful retirement strategy, there must be an intentional, focused, and realistic analysis of what life looks like after your career comes to a close. People on average are living longer and are able to remain healthy and active well into their sunset years. A well-designed plan can enable you to live comfortably and securely in retirement as you prepare for whatever the future may bring.

This book is a key element in beginning preparation for what should be the most enjoyable culmination of a job well done.

Jim Hagale
President, Bass Pro Shops and Cabela's, Retired

INTRODUCTION

"WE DON'T KNOW WHERE TO START."

Matt and Judy sat down in my office and began to tell me about their lives. Matt had worked thirty years at two different companies. Judy had been a teacher. They had just reached retirement age and felt clueless about where to begin planning financially for the years ahead. What I shared with Matt and Judy is what I'm going to share with you over the next several chapters.

I want you to have a great retirement. And I'm going to give you everything you need to get the retirement you've been dreaming about. I have been able to help my clients become well prepared for what happens when they stop working. I want you to be just as prepared as they are.

> **"We don't know where to start."**

Retirement is different these days. As Alan Gotthardt notes in *The Eternity Portfolio*:

> At one time in America, life was simple for those who lived to be retirees. He worked thirty-five to forty years for one company, and that company agreed to pay you a nice pension starting at age sixty-five and lasting the rest of your life. The average life expectancy for people at that time was

somewhere in the early seventies, so investing and inflation were not really much of a concern for the five to ten years on average retirement.[1]

For our parents, retirement meant switching from a paycheck to a pension check, setting up Social Security benefits, and maybe selling their small farm to supplement their retirement income.

The America that Gotthardt describes no longer exists. By retirement, most American workers have been employed by seven or eight companies, have no pension, and have participated in several different 401(k) plans. People are living much longer now than before, which means their days in retirement are lasting longer than expected.

This book answers the question, "How do I retire?" And it guides you through the steps as you get closer to retirement. The following pages help you evaluate your monthly income needs in retirement, maximize your Social Security benefits and investment returns, discover all of your income sources, understand the different investment options, and transfer your wealth to the next generation. Finally, this book helps you understand the key points of a financial plan so you can meet your retirement goals.

I encourage you to take notes and dog-ear pages that are most relevant to you. This is not a coffee table book. It's a working document to help you ask the right questions so you can maximize every financial resource available to you. Also, it's important to note that some of the sections address the tax treatment of various investments. Please remember this material is general in nature. Every situation is different, so contact your tax professional about your specific situation.

How Do I Retire? helps you assess where you are in regard to your retirement goals and discover a plan to reach those goals. Read the following pages slowly, and fill out all the worksheets so you can take this book to your financial advisor and use it as the foundation for a long and successful retirement.

You're going to love retirement.

Running with the call (Hab. 2:2),

Richard L. Baker

CHAPTER ONE
A STARTING POINT

"How do we know if we can retire?"

Judy told me this was the first thing she and her husband, Matt, talked about on the drive home from a coworker's retirement party. They'd worked for many years and had pretty good balances in their retirement accounts. Even so, they had no idea how to figure out if they could afford to retire.

Planning for retirement can seem like piecing together an intimidating puzzle. People often tell me they feel alone. They fear making costly mistakes. How can they know if their financial choices today mean sufficient income tomorrow? That's why I commend you for reading this book. My goal is to walk through these important decisions with you.

> **"How do we know if we can retire?"**

Imagine you're putting together a jigsaw puzzle. Where do you start? Typically, the border is the best place to begin because it helps frame the picture. In this chapter, you're going to take the first step in putting your retirement puzzle together. You're going to discover the retirement foundations you need to begin.

Keep these questions in mind:

- Am I emotionally ready to retire?
- What type of retirement am I going to have?
- What are my retirement goals?
- Barring an unexpected illness or accident, how long should I expect retirement to last?
- And how much will inflation affect my retirement income?

BE EMOTIONALLY READY TO RETIRE

When Matt and Judy met me for the first time, they were both excited and anxious about retirement. They were excited about having more time to relax and spend with family and hobbies. But they also were anxious about whether they could afford retirement. Some people wonder if they are emotionally ready to handle the life change that comes with retirement.

It's easy to understand these mixed feelings about retirement when you add them to other significant events in your life. Remember when you got married, had a baby, bought a house, or changed jobs? These were good times, but they also brought change, excitement, and fear. In the same way, retirement comes with life changes that can be both exciting and frightening.

Though many people say they wish they didn't have to work, the reality is there are good things about working – most notably, friendships with coworkers, a regular schedule, fulfillment, and a feeling of being valued.

For forty years or more, you've been going to work five days a week. Now, you know there's a Monday coming when you wake up as usual but aren't expected in the office, shop, or warehouse. I guarantee it will feel strange. Many of my clients tell me it can take up to a year for them to get comfortable with not going to work. This is normal.

Prepare yourself for the emotional change by thinking about how to retain the things you like about work. Write down ways to see your coworkers away from the office. Develop a regular schedule of activities to keep your mind engaged and your body active. And learn to plug in places where you're needed and valued.

MAKE GOALS FOR YOUR RETIREMENT

Planning for retirement involves more than saving money. In retirement, your financial focus changes. The way you manage your money in retirement is different from the way you manage it now. Instead of saving money to grow your retirement account, you have to figure out how to live off that retirement account as a substitute for your paycheck.

Let me shoot straight. You need your investments to grow enough so you can enjoy the same lifestyle in retirement that you enjoy now – and not run out of money. You do that by earning a consistent income stream (from investments) and making good financial decisions.

How much money will you need? To answer that question, you must decide what kind of retirement you want. You need to think through what your retirement actually looks like. What's your schedule? With whom do you plan to spend time? Where are you going to live? What hobbies or volunteer services are in your future? You may not have all the answers yet, but it's not too early to begin the thought process.

> "You need your investments to grow ... so you can enjoy retirement ... and not run out of money."

You can't hit a target if you can't see it. Retirement goals are the same way. You have to have them, preferably in written form, so you can see them and reach them. Everyone has different goals for retirement. And everyone has different expectations and dreams about life beyond the workplace.

To set your retirement goals, you need to get a pen, paper, and your significant other and set aside some time to dream out loud.

First, dream. What would you like to do each month? It's easier to work on it from a monthly perspective and then reduce it to bite-size weekly goals later. Do you want to fish, golf, or volunteer at your church once a week or twice a month?

Second, prioritize your dreams and write them down in the order of importance. Make them specific, set them within a time frame like Tuesday/Thursday mornings, and write down next to them how much you think they are going to cost.

Third, organize your dreams. Which dreams are seasonal or have time restraints? (For example, maybe the food bank isn't open on Fridays.) Break the dreams down into goals and a working weekly schedule.

Complete your retirement goals before moving on to the next chapter. Be able to answer the question, "What will a normal month in retirement look like for me?"

RETIREMENT MAY LAST LONGER THAN YOU THINK

Don't underestimate your longevity – or your spouse's. Over the last hundred years or so, life expectancy has risen dramatically in the U.S. In the year 1900, the average life expectancy was forty-nine years, but in 2017, the average life expectancy rose above seventy-eight years. A third of males and half of females in their fifties today will live to age ninety. Even more surprising, there is a fifty-fifty chance that one member of a sixty-five-year-old couple will live to age ninety-two.[1]

People are simply living longer than their parents did, and much longer than they financially planned to live. With the advances in medicine and technology, and more attention on healthy lifestyles, it is entirely possible that many retirees may live a lot longer than their parents or grandparents. This means a longer life to enjoy, but it also means you need enough money invested to provide income for a long retirement.

The following graph shows the probability of a sixty-five-year-old man, woman, and one member of a sixty-five-year-old couple living to different ages.

Probability of living from age 65 to…			
Age	Male	Female	Probability of one Spouse living
70	95%	96%	100%
75	88%	90%	99%
80	77%	80%	96%
85	60%	66%	86%
90	38%	46%	66%
95	16%	23%	35%

(Source: Joint Life Probability; Financial Architects LLC.)

At least one member of a sixty-five-year-old couple has more than a ninety percent chance of living to age eighty or beyond. And, shockingly, they have more than a fifty-fifty chance of reaching ninety years of age, and a one-in-three chance of living to ninety-five or older. While these represent "average" life expectancies, and you may not live that long, it's important to financially plan for that possibility.[2]

> **"You could spend a third of your life in retirement."**

I bring this up to say that you may need investments in place to provide income for twenty to thirty-five years because you could spend a third of your life in retirement. I cannot say this strongly enough: the longer you or your spouse lives, the longer your investments must grow so you don't outlive your money. The good news is that you might live long enough to have meaningful relationships with your great-grandchildren, but the challenge is making sure your retirement money lasts as long as you do.

If you are in good health and have a family history of longevity, your retirement plan should account for thirty or more years of monthly living expenses.

PLAN FOR INFLATION

Everything is more expensive. Inflation is simply the cost of goods and services getting more expensive over time. My parents were born in the late 1940s and remember prices of goods and services being much lower than today. My parents remember a loaf of bread priced at a quarter. Gasoline was eight cents a gallon. And for a nickel, you could buy a bottle of Coke or a candy bar. The reason these things are a lot more expensive today is because of inflation. Inflation affects every aspect of retirement, from the cost of a house to the cost of the hotdogs you grill in the back yard.

You may not know it, but you have been fighting inflation your whole life. It was easier to manage because you were working, and your income generally increased at the same rate. But in retirement, your income is somewhat fixed, and this poses a fresh set of challenges.

Your retirement plan needs to be flexible so you can adjust to the rising prices of your home, car, fuel, groceries, and healthcare. Many retirees tell me they are using a budget for the first time in their marriage out of necessity because they didn't plan for inflation.

Inflation rates 2000-2020*			
Year	Rate of Inflation	Year	Rate of Inflation
2000	3.40%	2011	3.00%
2001	2.80%	2012	1.70%
2002	1.60%	2013	1.50%
2003	2.30%	2014	0.80%
2004	2.70%	2015	0.70%
2005	3.40%	2016	2.10%
2006	3.20%	2017	2.10%
2007	2.80%	2018	1.90%
2008	3.80%	2019	2.30%
2009	-0.40%	2020	1.20%
2010	1.50%	Average	2.11%

*As of August 31, 2020

Let me give you an example that demonstrates the effects of annual inflation of three percent. Weekly groceries for your family that cost $50 today will cost $121 for the same items in thirty years if inflation continues at a three percent pace. That is 2.4 times more than today.

Another example is your friend who retired in 1990. Then, he was able to buy a loaf of bread for seventy cents. But in the year 2010, after he'd been retired for twenty years, he would have paid $1.36 for that same loaf.[3]

In the same way, inflation affects you in your future retirement years. The table nearby gives you an idea of what the prices of a few common items *could* be during your retirement at a three percent inflation rate.

Inflation Is Not Likely to Slow Down			
Item	Cost in 1985	Cost in 2021	At 3% inflation, projected cost in 2040
First class stamp[1]	$0.22	$0.55	$0.96
Loaf of bread[2]	$0.55	$1.49	$2.61
Movie ticket[3]	$3.55	$11.89	$20.85
New car[4]	$11,838	$42,258	$74,100

[1] United States Postal Service, www.usps.com (8/25/2021)
[2] U.S. Bureau of Labor Statistics, www.bls.gov (8/25/2021)
[3] Wehrenberg Theater, www.wehrenberg.com (8/25/2021)
[4] The People History, www.thepeoplehistory.com and mediaroom.kbb.com (8/25/2021)

Here is an example of how it should work. If you need $1,100 in two years to buy an item that costs $1,000 today, then the rate of return on your investments should be high enough to earn an additional $100 over two years. The temptation is to invest your retirement savings extremely conservatively to protect your nest egg, but doing so could hold back your investments from growing and staying ahead of inflation. Investing too conservatively could make your money lose purchasing power over time.

As you can see below in the hypothetical examples, the different retirement balances begin losing purchasing power quickly at three percent inflation. This shows what can happen to the purchasing power of your savings balance if it is not protected from inflation.

Your Shrinking Purchasing Power				
Annual Inflation Rate	Retirement Value	After 5 Years	After 15 Years	After 25 Years
3%	$500,000	$430,000	$320,000	$230,000
3%	$750,000	$640,000	$470,000	$350,000
3%	$1,000,000	$860,000	$630,000	$470,000

These examples are hypothetical mathematical principles for illustration only. A 3 percent annual inflation rate cannot be assumed or guaranteed. Actual results may vary.

Although these are just hypothetical examples, you can see that with inflation at three percent, your money's purchasing power will be cut in half in twenty-five years. That's why it's so important for your retirement investments to keep up with or exceed the actual inflation rate to avoid losing purchasing power late in retirement.

Larry Burkett writes, "For the majority of retirees, inflation is the most disastrous of all the circumstances they may face" because inflation "will eat the heart out of any retirement plan at a time when the retiree has little or no flexibility."[4] Since the overall cost of everyday living typically rises each year, your annual retirement income needs to increase each year as well.

You might be thinking, "That sounds scary. What can I do about inflation?" Keep three things in mind while you plan. First, when deciding how your retirement investments are going to be invested and who is going to manage them, know that your retirement income needs to perform well enough to keep pace with inflation year after year. Second, when you write out your retirement goals, plan to spend less than you can afford so you are not caught off guard later. Third, make spending decisions with retirement in mind, especially in regard to houses, vehicles, and other items that have long-term payments that could stretch into your retirement years.

A good investment plan lessens the impact of inflation. Rising costs are manageable if you plan for them beforehand.

KEY TAKEAWAYS

Prepare emotionally to retire.

Prepare yourself for emotional changes by thinking through how you may retain the things you like about work. Think through and write down ways to see your coworkers away from the office. Develop a regular schedule you can keep in retirement and think about plugging in where you feel fulfilled and valued. There are good things about work-life that are worth replacing during retirement.

Write down retirement goals.

You and your spouse need to set aside some time to dream out loud. Make a sample monthly activity schedule. Make your activities realistic and in order of importance. Dream big and then organize your dreams.

Estimate how long your retirement will last.

Don't underestimate your longevity – or your spouse's. People are simply living longer than their parents did, and much longer than they financially planned to live. Have a contingency plan for income in case you live much longer than you expect in retirement.

Plan for future inflation.

Plan for a continual increase in the prices of things you buy every month. Hire a good financial professional to manage your retirement investments in a way that keeps pace with inflation. Spend less than you make. Try not to purchase large ticket items late in your career so that you don't have loan payments that stretch into your retirement years.

QUESTIONS FOR PERSONAL OR GROUP STUDY

1. What do you need in order to feel happy and satisfied? What in your work-life contributes to your happiness? How can you retain these in retirement?
2. What retirement goals are important to you? Do you want to travel? Are you planning to live in your current home or in a vacation home? Are you planning to provide financially for your children or grandchildren?
3. How long do people in your family tend to live? How does that correlate with your lifespan, considering the advances in health and medical technology?
4. What examples of inflation have you seen in your life? How can you plan for future inflation?

CHAPTER TWO
YOUR MONTHLY SPENDING PLAN

"WE WERE A LITTLE TOO AMBITIOUS."

I talked with Tom and Stacey about completing a financial plan before they retired, but they didn't think they needed one. "We've got a fifteen-thousand-dollar cushion in our checking account, and we don't think we'll spend any more than our retirement income," they explained.

Six months later, they walked into my office. The first thing they said was, "We were a little too ambitious. Our checking account cushion is gone, and we bounced a check for the first time in years."

That cushion in their checking account seemed big to them. But in reality, without a spending plan, they were sure to run out of money. The good news is that this happened early in their retirement. They were able to make adjustments. We worked together on a spending plan, and they haven't had problems since.

Tom and Stacey needed a spending plan, and so will you. Fun always costs money – even retirement fun. You can have a long and financially stress-free retirement as long as you keep expenses aligned with income. That's where a spending plan comes in. Let's identify four aspects of a spending plan that help you reach your goals and stay in the black, too:

- First, the percentage of your full-time salary needed in retirement
- Second, preparing for multiple income sources

- Third, understanding that different chapters of retirement have different expenses
- Fourth, calculating future monthly expenses for day one, year ten, and year twenty

Moving to the beach, spending your days crappie fishing, playing golf, and learning to park a motorhome all have one thing in common: these activities cost money. Chapter 1 explained how to match each retirement goal with an estimated cost. The next step in the retirement-plan process is to calculate the total monthly income you are going to need to make these dreams come true.

This is the point where I hear some people at the end of their careers say, "I don't need to calculate my expenses. I'll adjust my spending to whatever income rolls in."

In a perfect world, that might work, but I have never seen it work in real life. There are too many large fixed costs like housing or healthcare expenses that are not flexible enough to allow you to "wing it." Your lifestyle is going to change, and you might need to make adjustments to your spending *before* you retire to accommodate the lifestyle you expect to have in retirement.

HOW MUCH WILL YOUR RETIREMENT COST?

One of the first questions people looking at retirement ask me is, "Can we afford to retire?" The answer depends on how long you live and what kind of lifestyle you plan to have in retirement.

Financial planning experts often suggest that, in retirement, you need between seventy percent and one hundred percent of the annual gross salary you earned during your final year of fulltime employment. Of course, the exact percentage depends on a number of factors, such as your lifestyle level, health, and level of debt.

But this is a good rule of thumb. Later in this chapter, we look at how you can focus on your current expenses and decide which of these expenses continue after you retire. Unless you're planning an extravagant lifestyle in retirement, your living expenses generally go down in retirement because you have lower taxes and are no longer contributing to your 401(k).

WHERE WILL THE INCOME COME FROM?

There is give and take at the start of retirement. You get more time and flexibility since you're no longer working every day. But you also take on more financial responsibilities. For instance, it is now up to you to make sure you get paid each month.

Many people experience a change in going from one paycheck when they were working to four or five sources of income in retirement. They may even receive these payments on different days of the month. It's all manageable, but getting used to it takes time.

As an example, let's say you and your spouse are working, and your combined annual income is $85,000 a year. You plan to live on about seventy percent of that amount during retirement. That means you need $60,000 in the first year of retirement. That $60,000 might come from multiple sources, such as Social Security, employer pension plans, or farm or other investment properties, but a lot of it will come from the money you saved in your employer's retirement savings plan.

It might look like the illustration below. The left column shows it as an annual amount, and the right side shows it on a monthly basis.

Annual vs. Monthly Income		
Income Source	$60,000 Annual Income	$5,000 Monthly Income
Spouse #1 Social Security	$21,600	$1,800
Spouse #2 Social Security	$16,800	$1,400
Pension	$2,400	$200
Retirement Savings Withdrawal	$19,200	$1,600

Often, new retirees struggle to track monthly income since it arrives from four different sources on four different days of the month. It is a little different from the one or two paychecks that came like clockwork into your checking account on standard days of the month. But take heart. You'll adjust.

THE THREE CHAPTERS OF RETIREMENT

Not every year of retirement is the same. You can guarantee that the last few years of your retirement will look much different than the first few years. It might be helpful to think of your retirement in three chapters: early retirement, middle retirement, and late retirement.

The chapters likely are going to be unequal in length and unequal in cost, so you want to make your plans, especially your financial plans, accordingly. The length of each chapter depends on the age you retire and your health. Each person has a unique retirement profile, but most people experience these three chapters.

> **"Not every year of your retirement is the same..."**

The Early Retirement Chapter, often experienced during ages sixty-two to seventy, is probably the most active and most expensive chapter because you are relatively young and healthy. This chapter has more of a vacation feel, which comes with higher travel and entertainment expenses. These expenses level off after a few years and, as a result, your monthly expenses become more predictable. During this chapter, you adjust to not receiving a steady paycheck, and you start managing your own monthly income.

Sometimes, healthy retirees with more free time on their hands are tempted to go on a spending spree during this chapter of their lives. To guard against this, you shouldn't make any huge purchases until you see if they fit into your retirement plan. One way to manage new expenses in early retirement is to take a part-time or seasonal job, or start a business that gives you flexible work hours and some additional income.

At the beginning of this chapter, you make two major decisions: when to start claiming Social Security benefits, and where you and your spouse get health insurance. If one or both of you aren't yet old enough to enroll in Medicare, then you need to see if you qualify for Medicaid, or you need to purchase private health insurance.

For many retirees, *The Middle Retirement Chapter*, often experienced during ages seventy to eighty, is the longest and least expensive chapter. Many people begin to tire of the travel and activities in which they engaged during their early retirement years. Thus, they stay closer to home and live a more a settled life.

A lot of retirees in this chapter see their focus change to maintaining good health and staying independent. Most of my clients in the middle chapter reduce exotic travel and spend more relaxed time with their loved ones. Travel begins to focus on visiting grandchildren and other family and friends. Some retirees downsize their houses and vehicles. They simplify all around. Relationships become more important than new experiences.

In this middle chapter, you also claim Social Security benefits, because age seventy is the last year the federal government rewards you for delaying. At age seventy-two, you have to start taking Required Minimum Distributions (RMDs) from your retirement accounts, such as profit-sharing, 401(k), 403(b), 457(b), and Roth 401(k) plans, as well as from traditional IRAs.

Finally, you may want to update your will or estate plan while you're still healthy and mentally capable. This is a great time to decide how your money and assets are distributed after you pass away. It's also a good time to set up a financial and healthcare power of attorney in the event you need someone else to make decisions for you.

The beginning of *The Late Retirement Chapter*, often experienced beyond age eighty, seems to sneak up on retirees. It may be a health scare that signals the onset of this chapter. Even so, many say this final chapter in retirement is the best one. Contentment and gratitude are easier when retirees reach this stage and bond with family and friends in more relaxing ways.

A great deal of time is spent sharing experiences and wisdom with grandchildren and great-grandchildren. Significantly more time is spent at the doctor's office as well. That's because retirees may confront serious health issues. Many of my clients find they have significantly less energy. They also come to grips with being more financially and physically limited than in earlier retirement years.

Late in this chapter, many of my clients see a sudden increase in expenses for comfort, security, and healthcare. Medicare pays some of these expenses, but retirees still need to plan for co-payments, deductibles, prescriptions, expenses related to independent or assisted-living facilities, or home health aides. During this chapter, you need to be strategic with your income in order to meet your needs and, hopefully, have something to leave your loved ones.

Each chapter of your retirement is different. If you're fortunate enough to enjoy a lengthy retirement, your income may need to cover expenses for three decades, or even longer. How you save and spend determines where you live, and your quality of life.

If you keep the unique features of the three retirement chapters in mind, you'll be better prepared with your budget along the way. Make sure your retirement income has some flexibility because expenses vary greatly between the early, middle, and late retirement chapters. Spend some time at the beginning of each retirement chapter to evaluate and adjust your income to reflect the change in expenses.

CALCULATING YOUR MONTHLY EXPENSES

To plan for your retirement chapters, you must understand and control your expenses. It's important to know as soon as possible if your expected retirement income is enough to meet your needs. Your monthly expenses in retirement dictate how much monthly income you need. Sometimes, it's difficult to predict future expenses. However, calculating your current spending gives you a good idea of what your retirement spending may look like.

To calculate your monthly income needs, you must first figure out what you're spending now. Take time right away to fill out the next worksheet, titled "Calculating Your Monthly Expenses." Don't skip over this important step. It's important to know exactly what you're spending now so that you'll know what you need to maintain your lifestyle in retirement.

It may not seem important to write out how much you spend on birthday presents, movie tickets, or boat fuel, but if those things are part of your normal spending now, they are likely to continue in retirement. These seemingly small items help you get a clearer picture of what you might spend during retirement.

Don't underestimate the actual cost of your retirement lifestyle by missing some expenses. Doing this step helps reduce the potential for financial surprises that could severely constrain your retirement plans. Take the time to complete this worksheet. This is too important for guesswork.

A good way to start is to look through the last three months of receipts, along with your checking account and credit card statements. Find a pattern in your spending. You may be surprised to see where all your money goes. Notice that there are two columns on the "Calculating Your Monthly Expenses" worksheet. The first column is for current expenses, and the second column is for expenses after you retire.

HOW DO I RETIRE? 17

Worksheet "A"
Calculating Your Monthly Expenses

ITEM	Monthly Expenses PreRetirement	Monthly Expenses in Retirement	ITEM	Monthly Expenses PreRetirement	Monthly Expenses in Retirement
Home Mortgage/Rent	$	$	Sports/Hobbies	$	$
Property Taxes	$	$	Pets: Cost, Food, License	$	$
Homeowner's/Renter's Insurance	$	$	Credit Card Payments	$	$
Gas, Electricity, Fuel (Home)	$	$	Other Loans/Notes Payments	$	$
Trash/Water/Sewer	$	$	Life Insurance Premiums	$	$
Homeowner's Assn. Dues	$	$	Personal Property, State, Fed Income Tax	$	$
Home Maintenance/Repair	$	$	Savings	$	$
Cell phone/TV/Internet	$	$	Investments	$	$
Auto Payments/Public Transp.	$	$	Other _____	$	$
Gas, Oil, Tires	$	$			
Auto Maintenance	$	$			
Auto Insurance	$	$			
License(s)	$	$	**Total NonMedical Expenses**	$ _____ (A1)	$ _____ (A2)
Groceries	$	$			
Clothing	$	$	**HEALTHCARE**		
Laundry/Dry Cleaning/Gym	$	$	Medical: Eyeglasses, hearing aids	$	$
Church/Charities	$	$	Dental	$	$
Vacation Fund	$	$	Drugs/Medical Supplies	$	$
Holiday/Birthday/Anniversary Fund	$	$	Health Insurance	$	$
Membership Dues	$	$			
Subscriptions (Paper, Magazines)	$	$	**Total Medical Expenses**	$ _____ (A3)	$ _____ (A4)
Entertainment	$	$		A1	A2
Dining Out	$	$		+A3	+A4
Allowances	$	$	**TOTAL MONTHLY EXPENSES**	$ ======	$ ======

Download a printable version of this worksheet via highstreet.press/retire.

Consider these important steps:

Step One. Use the column on the left to write down monthly expenses. Complete the entire current expense section before moving on. Do your best to estimate what you usually spend on birthdays, Christmas gifts and decorations, and any other similar expenses. Don't worry if you don't have exact records of your spending in a particular category. Just estimate until you find more accurate data. You can go back and edit anytime.

If a category has fluctuating monthly expenses, like birthday gifts or utility bills, estimate what you spend over the whole year and divide that total by twelve for an average monthly expense. Similarly, if you pay a bill quarterly (like many do for car insurance), multiply it by four and divide the yearly amount by twelve to get the monthly average. Lastly, figure monthly expenses for the whole household, not just for you.

Step Two. The column on the right is for current expenses that continue after retirement. These are the expenses that stay the same every month whether you are retired or not, such as rent or mortgage payments, water, sewer, real estate taxes, cable television, cell phone, car payments, healthcare payments, and anything else that continues after you stop working.

Step Three. Look over your current expenses in the left-hand column and decide if they continue when you retire, or if they decline. For example, you still have transportation expenses after you retire, but likely they decrease because you're not commuting to work any longer. Your clothing expenses may decrease as well. On the other hand, some expenses may rise in retirement, like medical expenses, especially if you currently enjoy a generous employer health plan. Medicare helps, but it doesn't cover everything.

> "Medicare ... doesn't cover everything."

Step Four. After you have written down the expenses that continue into retirement, go back through the column on the right and jot down an estimated cost for your retirement entertainment goals, which may include golf, fishing, or travel. Don't try to adjust for inflation yet; we tackle that later.

Step Five. Now, add up all the columns to get a total monthly expense.

HOW DID THE MONTHLY EXPENSES CALCULATION WORK OUT?

While anything but enjoyable, this exercise is well worth it for getting a snapshot of your current and future expenses. If your estimated retirement expenses are more than the estimated income you plan to have (which is common), you have three choices: (1) increase your income, (2) decrease your expenses, or (3) delay your retirement date until some of the expenses go away.

> "Do what you can afford."

The worksheet surprises many people – and perhaps it surprised you. You may be asking yourself questions like, "Do we really eat out that much?" If you want to perform some self-analysis, use the optional guide below to see if your monthly expenses are out of whack in any category:

Sample Guidelines for Retirement Expense Percentages	
Church/Charities	10%
Taxes	7%
Housing, upkeep, utilities, furniture	25%
Food at home	5%
Food away from home	5%
Transportation, insurance, maintenance, fuel	15%
Other insurance	5%
Entertainment	5%
Medical/Dental	13%
All other expenses	10%

These are general guidelines to help you work out your retirement budget by comparing your expenses with average expenses in these categories. No judgment here. Do what you can afford.

ADJUSTING FUTURE INCOME FOR INFLATION

Sadly, these expense amounts, based on today's prices, won't stay the same throughout your retirement. Most of us understand at some level that a dollar buys less in the future than what it purchases today. So, we must estimate what your future income needs to be to keep pace with rising prices. To do that, we need to adjust your current expenses for inflation.

This section helps you look at expenses today and estimate how they might increase over time. This enables you to know when you have saved enough money to retire. And it helps you make big purchasing decisions late in your career that could affect your finances in retirement.

Calculating your inflation-adjusted monthly expenses in ten years

(1) Using information from Worksheet A, "Calculating Your Monthly Expenses," move on to Worksheet B, "Calculating Monthly Expenses in 10 Years." Even a reasonable rate of inflation pushes up your expenses over time. This worksheet shows you how much your retirement income might need to increase to keep pace with future inflation.

Worksheet B assumes an annual average inflation rate of three percent for non-healthcare expenses and assumes an annual average inflation rate of seven percent for healthcare expenses. If you have a fixed-rate mortgage, you do not need to include this amount because it stays the same over the years, but don't forget to include your mortgage payment in the total. *These percentages are for illustration only. Actual inflation rates may differ.*

(2) Take the total from line A2 (non-healthcare expenses) from Worksheet A and place the amount at the top left-hand side of Worksheet B.

(3) Next, take the total from line A4 (healthcare expenses) from Worksheet A and place the amount in the middle of the left-hand side of Worksheet B.

(4) Now, working left to right, take these totals, multiply them by the inflation factor, and write the total on the corresponding right-hand side of the page.

(5) Add your inflation-adjusted non-healthcare expenses to the inflation-adjusted healthcare expenses to estimate your expenses in the tenth year of retirement.

Worksheet B
Calculating Monthly Expenses in 10 Years

Section One

	From Worksheet "A" Line #A2	10 Year Inflation Factor	Non-Health Expenses In 10 Years Adjusted for Inflation
Total Monthly Expenses (other than healthcare)	_____	X 1.34 (3%)	_____(A)

	From Worksheet "A" Line #A4	10 Year Inflation Factor	Health Expenses In 10 Years Adjusted for Inflation
Total Monthly Healthcare Expenses	_____	X 1.97 (7%)	_____(B)

Section Two

Non-Healthcare Inflation Adjusted Expenses (A)   _____

Healthcare Inflation Adjusted Expenses (B)   + ========================

Total Monthly Expenses in 10 Years, Adjusted for Inflation (A+B)   _____

Download a printable version of this worksheet via highstreet.press/retire.

Calculating your inflation-adjusted monthly expenses in twenty years

(1) Using information from Worksheet A, "Calculating Your Monthly Expenses," move on to Worksheet C, "Calculating Monthly Expenses in 20 Years." Even a reasonable rate of inflation pushes up your expenses over time. This shows it's necessary to raise your retirement income to keep pace with future inflation.

Worksheet C assumes an annual average inflation rate of three percent for non-healthcare expenses, and it assumes an annual average inflation rate of seven percent for healthcare expenses. As before, your fixed-rate mortgage need not be included, but make sure to include it in the total.

> "... raise your retirement income to keep pace with future inflation."

(2) Take the total from line A2 (non-healthcare expenses) from Worksheet A and place it on the top left-hand side of Worksheet C.

(3) Next, take the total from line A4 (healthcare expenses) from Worksheet A and place it in the middle of the left-hand side of Worksheet C.

(4) Now, working left to right, take these totals, multiply them by the inflation factor, and put the total on the corresponding right-hand side of the page.

(5) Add your inflation-adjusted non-healthcare expenses to the inflation-adjusted healthcare expenses to estimate your expenses in the twentieth year of retirement.

Worksheet C
Calculating Monthly Expenses in 20 Years

Section One

	From Worksheet "A" Line #A2	20 Year Inflation Factor	Non-Health Expenses In 20 Years Adjusted for Inflation
Total Monthly Expenses (other than healthcare)	_____	X 1.81 (3%)	_____ (A)

	From Worksheet "A" Line #A4	20 Year Inflation Factor	Health Expenses In 20 Years Adjusted for Inflation
Total Monthly Healthcare Expenses	_____	X 3.87 (7%)	_____ (B)

Section Two

Non-Healthcare Inflation Adjusted Expenses (A)   _____

Healthcare Inflation Adjusted Expenses (B)   + ======================

Total Monthly Expenses in 20 Years, Adjusted for Inflation (A+B) _____

Download a printable version of this worksheet via highstreet.press/retire.

You need flexibility in your retirement plan to meet rising monthly expenses. Inflation is a significant factor in determining how much money you need each month in the different years of retirement. You should strive to keep expenses in line, while at the same time managing investments so they earn enough to keep up with the yearly rise of inflation.

It is impossible to predict future inflation rates because they have fluctuated widely throughout history. For instance, in 1979, during the Jimmy Carter administration, inflation was 11.3 percent, but in 2009, during the George W. Bush administration, inflation registered at - 0.4 percent.[1]

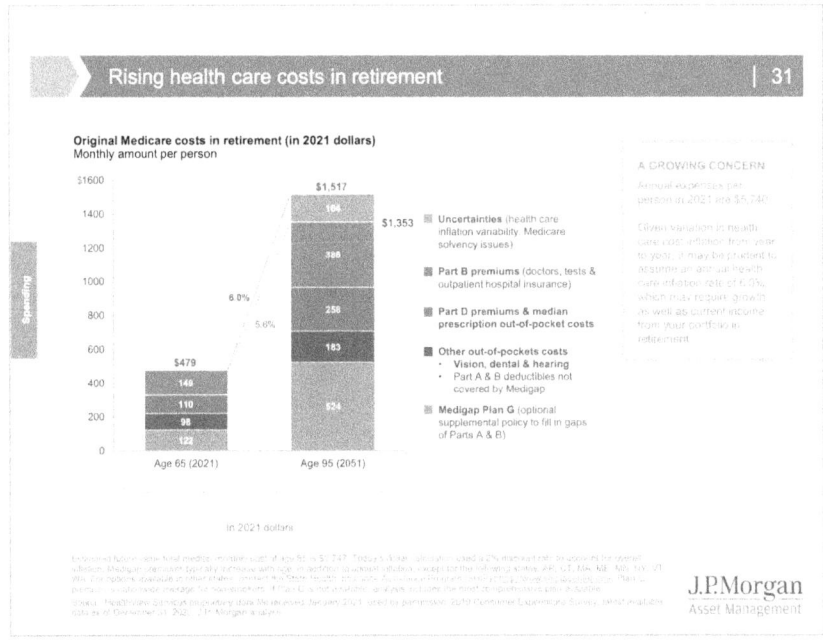

Rising health care costs chart created by J.P. Morgan, used by permission. Download a printable version via highstreet.press/retire.

On Worksheets B and C, I used three-percent inflation for non-healthcare expenses, but seven percent for medical expenses. That's because of the sudden increase in medical expenses the last few years, as you can see from the chart above. Because medical expenses are outpacing normal inflation, I felt we needed to separate them. I believe this approach is more accurate, but keep in mind that these are only estimations.

Another useful tool to estimate inflation is the Bureau of Labor Statistics' inflation calculator online at bls.gov/data/inflation_calculator.htm. Use this webpage to calculate your purchasing power over different time periods based on historical inflation rates. Of course, the calculator doesn't predict the future, but it can prove helpful in estimating the future income you need.

KEY TAKEAWAYS

Decide how much of your salary you need in retirement.

No matter how you plan to enjoy retirement, it's going to cost money. Take the time to figure out where you stand by comparing expenses and income.

Prepare for multiple income sources.

Get ready mentally to receive several smaller checks each month rather than one or two larger paychecks. It comes to feel normal after a few months if you pattern your thought process now.

Figure out which retirement chapter you're in.

Not every year of retirement is the same. There are three different seasons, or chapters. Think through the different aspects of each chapter and prepare accordingly.

Calculate future monthly expenses.

Look through the last three months of receipts, along with your checking account and credit card statements. Find a pattern in your spending. Use Worksheets A, B, and C to calculate potential monthly expenses on retirement day one, and in ten and twenty years adjusted for inflation. You can reach your retirement goals as long as you keep expenses aligned with income. Your retirement dreams can become a reality if you manage monthly expenses well.

QUESTIONS FOR PERSONAL OR GROUP STUDY

1. How much of your current net (take-home) paycheck will you need when you retire? What expenses will no longer exist after you stop working?
2. How does getting several smaller checks each month in retirement, rather than the one or two large paychecks now, work with the way you pay your bills? Do you need to keep extra money in your checking account as a buffer? How will multiple checks affect the way you balance your checking account?
3. What changes do you anticipate as you pass from *The Early Retirement Chapter* to *The Middle Retirement Chapter*? Do you plan to move closer to your children and grandchildren? What changes do you anticipate as you pass from *The Middle Retirement Chapter* to *The Late Retirement Chapter*? How might you adjust for becoming less mobile?
4. What category of monthly expenses surprised you the most? Does that category need adjusting?

CHAPTER THREE
GETTING THE MOST OUT OF SOCIAL SECURITY

"I can't get a straight answer out of anyone over there!"

She was more frazzled than I had ever seen her. Judy stopped by unannounced, walked into one of my conference rooms, and threw some papers on the table. She had just come from the Social Security office and was completely confused. She said, "I can't get a straight answer out of anyone over there!" I watched Judy go from confusion to anger.

Social Security is not welfare. It is *your* money, which the federal government took from *your* paycheck, to provide for *your* retirement. Take as much of it as you can.

In this chapter, we discuss the basic elements of Social Security:

- Social Security benefit eligibility
- Different strategies for when to start claiming benefits
- How your continued employment could affect Social Security benefits
- Social Security cost-of-living adjustments (COLAs)
- How your benefits are taxed
- Who qualifies for spousal benefits
- The possibility that the Social Security Administration may run out of money

This chapter alone is worth the price of the book. The Social Security system, like many government-run services, is a complicated mess. As

Judy discovered, it can be difficult to navigate unless you're prepared to ask the right questions. Before you sit down with a Social Security administrator, you need to understand what's best for you. So, let's get ready for that meeting.

WHAT IS SOCIAL SECURITY?

Before you learn to work Social Security to your greatest advantage, it helps to know the system's background and original intent. President Franklin D. Roosevelt signed Executive Order No. 6757 in June 1934, which created the Committee on Economic Security (renamed the Social Security Administration in 1946). Thus began what we know today as Social Security.

The new committee began designing a system of social insurance, with a primary emphasis on "assisting Americans with unemployment and old age insurance."[1] The federal government began collecting Social Security taxes in January 1937 and started paying retirement income benefits that same month.[2] It is now the U.S. government's single largest program.

Social Security retirement checks feel a lot like company pensions. While your parents and previous generations relied on their employer-provided pension plans for steady retirement income, most people today no longer have that luxury. That's because most companies abandoned pricey pension plans years ago. But Social Security retirement benefits are similar to a pension in that they provide a person with a consistent income stream backed by the U.S. government. Whether you're single, married, divorced, or widowed, the foundation for your retirement income will be your Social Security benefits.

> "The foundation for your retirement income will be your Social Security benefits."

Social Security *is* a trusted foundation to your future income, but it won't make you rich. Few retirees can live on Social Security benefits alone since these benefits are intended to supplement their retirement, not fully fund it. At full retirement age, your Social Security benefit is only designed to replace about forty percent of your pre-retirement income.

The amount of your Social Security benefit generally is based on your age and lifetime earnings record. To be eligible to receive Social Security retirement checks, you or your spouse must have worked forty quarters, or ten years, during which you paid Social Security taxes. The forty quarters qualify you for benefits, but it is your thirty-five years of highest earnings that the Social Security Administration (SSA) uses to calculate the amount of your income benefit.[3] If you work longer than thirty-five years, the SSA replaces a lower-earning year with a higher-earning year.

There are special rules for teachers, farmers, military service men and women, railroad workers, the self-employed, and international workers. Also, some nonprofit organizations, as well as federal, state, and local government employees, may qualify for benefits with fewer qualifying years. It's wise to go to the Social Security Administration's website (ssa.gov) to ensure the accuracy of the SSA's record of your annual earnings. Compare the SSA's statement of your earnings against the earnings shown on your W-2 forms for the same years. If there are mistakes in the SSA records that could lower your benefits, report them immediately.

In 2020, the average monthly Social Security benefit paid to a single person was about $1,500. The average retired couple had a combined benefit of about $2,600 per month.[4] Though you may be a high-income earner, there are restrictions on how much you may collect, even if you paid more in Social Security taxes than you'll ever get back. If you started receiving benefits at age seventy in 2021, your maximum Social Security benefit is just under $3,900 per month.[5]

Retirees' number one fear is that they'll outlive their money. Your Social Security retirement benefit should ease some of that fear because it's designed to last a lifetime. It's the starting point for calculating your retirement income because it's a guaranteed income stream. It's also a dependable income that offers spousal protection in case the breadwinning spouse dies first. In addition, there is some inflation protection thanks to annual cost-of-living increases. Remember, it's *your* money. Get as much of it as you can.

BENEFIT ELIGIBILITY

What does it take to be eligible for Social Security retirement benefits? A person is eligible for Social Security retirement benefits if they have worked long enough to earn "40 work credits throughout their working lifetime."[6] Only the government could make something so simple so difficult to understand.

A work credit is earned when a person is employed and makes at least

$1,170 in a single fiscal quarter (January – March, April – June, July – September, or October – December). Forty quarters roughly equate to ten years of work. So, if you have worked steadily for ten years or longer, you're eligible to receive Social Security retirement benefits.

If you have worked more than the necessary forty quarters, the Social Security Administration bases your benefit amount on the average of the highest thirty-five years of earnings you've had Social Security taxes withheld from your paycheck. If you have worked fewer than thirty-five years, had long periods of unemployment, worked part-time, or worked some years with low earnings, this could negatively affect your benefits calculation.

If you have not worked forty quarters, you may still be eligible for benefits if your spouse worked forty quarters. You also may be eligible if you are divorced from an eligible worker, if you were married to that worker for at least ten years and have not remarried. There's more about spousal benefits later in this chapter.

If you're unsure whether you have worked forty quarters or are on track to do so, call the Social Security Administration at 1-800-772-1213 or visit the SSA online at ssa.gov.

CLAIMING STRATEGIES

The ultimate goal is to file for benefits that maximize the total lifetime benefits you receive. The perfect age to start Social Security income is different for each person. People who have a shorter life expectancy might receive higher total lifetime Social Security benefits by starting Social Security income at an earlier age. Others, who enjoy good health, are working, and have family members who have lived into their late eighties or longer, may find that delaying the start of income benefits is their best approach. Still others may not have a choice because they need the income at an earlier age.

There are several factors to consider when deciding when to claim Social Security, such as your current age/health, your family's longevity, whether you plan to keep working from ages sixty-two to seventy, retirement goals, and whether you have other funds available to bridge the gap until your full retirement age (FRA).

Many Americans think the normal retirement age to receive Social Security benefits is sixty-five, and it was for those born before 1943. But as a result of the Social Security Amendments Act of 1983, the "full retirement age" is no longer sixty-five, but on a sliding scale depending on a person's year of birth. Full retirement age, as determined by the Social Security Administration, is when you're eligible to receive one hundred percent of your full retirement benefit (also called the *primary insurance amount* or PIA on some forms).

See the chart below to find your full retirement age. Note how claiming benefits early (at age sixty-two) or delaying benefits to age seventy permanently affects your monthly income.

Age/Benefit Percentages				
Year of birth	Full retirement age (FRA)	Age 62 benefit	FRA benefit	Age 70 benefit
1943-54	66	75.00%	100%	132.00%
1955	66 and 2 months	74.17%	100%	130.67%
1956	66 and 4 months	73.33%	100%	129.33%
1957	66 and 6 months	72.50%	100%	128.00%
1958	66 and 8 months	71.67%	100%	126.67%
1959	66 and 10 months	70.83%	100%	125.33%
1960 & later	67	70.00%	100%	124.00%

A married couple has several different options for claiming Social Security retirement benefits and spousal benefits. As a matter of fact, the Social Security Administration says there are ten thousand to forty thousand different benefit-claiming age options depending on the respective birth years for a married couple.[7]

The amount of your Social Security benefits is based on how high your earnings were during your working career and the age when you start taking income. A qualifying person can begin receiving benefits as early as age sixty-two, but the monthly benefit amount is less than could be claimed at full retirement age. *Taking your benefit earlier than your FRA permanently reduces your monthly income and does not increase when you reach full retirement age.*

> "Taking your benefit earlier than your FRA permanently reduces your monthly income and does not increase when you reach full retirement age."

After your sixty-second birthday, your monthly benefit amount increases slightly for each month you wait to start receiving income benefits. As mentioned earlier, your full retirement age (FRA) is when you get one hundred percent of your projected income benefit.

Further, your Social Security benefit increases eight percent per year for every year you delay Social Security benefits between your FRA and your seventieth birthday. There is no advantage in delaying past age seventy; the eight percent annual increase stops there. Put another way, at age seventy you receive your maximum Social Security retirement benefit.

Remember, the goal is to take as much total Social Security income as you can in your lifetime. Delaying the start of income benefits may increase not only your monthly income but your lifetime income, depending on how long you live.

Below, I've included a hypothetical example of the total benefits a person would earn in his or her lifetime by starting to receive Social Security income at different ages. The example assumes a person stops working at age sixty-two and has an FRA of age sixty-six with an FRA benefit of $2,000 a month. It also includes no cost-of-living increases. This is only an illustration; individual results vary.

Age/Total Income Example			
Monthly benefit	Total income at age 80	Total income at age 85	Total income at age 90
Age 62: $1,500	$324,000	$414,000	$504,000
Age 66: $2,000	$336,000	$456,000	$576,000
Age 70: $2,640	$316,000	$475,000	$633,600

As you can see, the total amount of lifetime benefits differs greatly based on the age a person starts receiving Social Security income.

Simply put, if you start taking your benefit income earlier than your full retirement age, you receive a smaller monthly amount, but you receive it for a longer period of time. If you wait to start your benefit income until your FRA or later, you receive a larger monthly income amount, but receive it for a shorter period of time.

We can't know exactly how long we'll live. However, we can make reasonable estimates by looking at our family histories and longevities, and by considering the probabilities of living to a certain age. Take a look at the chart below:

Lifespan Probability

Probability of 62-year-olds living at least to …	Age 80	Age 90
62-year-old male	61 percent	22 percent
62-year-old female	71 percent	33 percent
At least one person of a 62-year-old couple	89 percent	48 percent[8]

There's roughly a fifty-fifty chance that you or your spouse will live past age ninety. Just looking at the high probability of living past age eighty – and the reasonable chance of living past ninety – may convince you to wait until your full retirement age, or even to age seventy, before starting to take Social Security retirement benefits. But keep this significant point in mind: you have to have enough money and a flexible enough portfolio to cover your expenses until you start taking these benefits.

> "It may make more sense to wait until your full retirement age, or even age 70, to starting taking your Social Security benefits."

Let's look at two different options for starting benefits:

Option one: Wait until your full retirement age or even later if …

- You have other income to cover monthly expenses
- You plan to keep working
- You expect to live to age eighty-five or older

Option two: Start taking payments as soon as you're eligible (age sixty-two for most people) if …

- You've finished working and have no other income options to cover immediate expenses
- You have serious health issues that don't allow you to work
- You have a family history of serious health issues
- Your current expenses are more than your income and you need every dollar you can get to make ends meet
- You think you won't live past age eighty
- You prefer to take the benefit checks early in order to dollar-cost-average them into an investment portfolio

To look more closely at your situation, visit the Social Security Administration's website (ssa.gov) or call 1-800-772-1213 to request a statement with your Earnings Benefit Estimate.

CONTINUING TO WORK WHILE ELIGIBLE FOR SOCIAL SECURITY BENEFITS

For various reasons, some people continue to work after they retire. My uncle Ron retired after twenty-five years as a physician's assistant but got bored after a few months at home. He started driving a truck for our local blood bank and continued for eighteen years. If you decide to work full-time or part-time after age sixty-two, be aware that it may affect your Social Security benefits.

Delaying benefits and working past age sixty-two enhance your future income amounts since you continue to pay into Social Security. However, if you start taking Social Security benefits between age sixty-two and your full retirement age, and you continue to work, Social Security penalizes you if you make over a certain amount.

For example, in 2021, your Social Security benefits would have been reduced if you made over $18,960 that year.[9] If you're younger than full retirement age, and if you're working and collecting benefits, the Social Security Administration deducts $1 from your benefits for every $2 you make above the annual limit.

Let's say you're sixty-two and taking $20,000 from Social Security, but you make another $20,000 at a job. The Social Security Administration taxes you $10,000 on top of your regular taxes. I think this is ridiculous since it's your money that you paid into Social Security, but no one asked me.

In the calendar year you reach full retirement age, SSA deducts $1 from your benefits for every $3 you make over that year's annual limit.[10] Social Security stops penalizing you for working *and* collecting benefits the month you reach full retirement age.

To get around this, you either have to not work from age sixty-two until your full retirement age, or you have to work and not take Social Security benefits. Once you reach full retirement age, all bets are off. You can work and make as much as you like without being penalized by the SSA.

COST-OF-LIVING ADJUSTMENTS (COLAS)

Once you start taking Social Security benefits, your monthly benefit amount never goes down. It could go up, however, thanks to cost-of-living adjustments (COLAs). Social Security retirement benefits are indexed for inflation, so they increase as the cost of living rises each year. It is an automatic annual cost-of-living raise equal to the percentage increase in the Consumer Price Index for Urban Wage Earners and Clerical Workers (CPI-W), which changes year to year.

Automatic Cost-of-Living Adjustments Received since 1975

Date	Percent	Date	Percent	Date	Percent
July 1975	8.0%	January 1992	3.7%	January 2008	2.3%
July 1976	6.4%	January 1993	3.0%	January 2009	5.8%
July 1977	5.9%	January 1994	2.6%	January 2010	0.0%
July 1978	6.5%	January 1995	2.8%	January 2011	0.0%
July 1979	9.9%	January 1996	2.6%	January 2012	3.6%
July 1980	14.3%	January 1997	2.9%	January 2013	1.7%
July 1981	11.2%	January 1998	2.1%	January 2014	1.5%
July 1982	7.4%	January 1999	1.3%	January 2015	1.7%
January 1984	3.5%	January 2000	2.5%*	January 2016	0.0%
January 1985	3.5%	January 2001	3.5%	January 2017	0.3%
January 1986	3.1%	January 2002	2.6%	January 2018	2.0%
January 1987	1.3%	January 2003	1.4%	January 2019	2.8%
January 1988	4.2%	January 2004	2.1%	January 2020	1.6%
January 1989	4.0%	January 2005	2.7%	January 2021	1.3%
January 1990	4.7%	January 2006	4.1%		
January 1991	5.4%	January 2007	3.3%		

*The COLA for December 1999 was originally determined as 2.4 percent based on CPIs published by the Bureau of Labor Statistics. Pursuant to Public Law 106-554, however, this COLA is effectively now 2.5 percent.[11]

There is no way to project future COLA increases because the CPI-W fluctuates greatly, as you can see in the chart above. Since 1975, the average annual COLA has been about 3.9 percent. COLA increases help monthly benefits maintain their purchasing power by rising with inflation. One frustrating thing about COLAs, however, is that the increase SSA gives you turns out to be the same amount Medicare raises its rates, which are deducted from your Social Security check. So, it's a wash, not a raise.

TAXES AND SOCIAL SECURITY BENEFITS

Your Social Security benefits may be taxable. The Social Security Administration says that nearly forty percent of Social Security recipients have to pay income taxes on their benefits.[12] You have to pay federal taxes if your overall income exceeds specific limits. This usually affects people who have significant income in addition to their Social Security benefits.

> "Forty percent of Social Security recipients have to pay income taxes on their benefits."

These income limits change from year to year, so consult your tax preparer to determine what amount of taxes should be withheld from your monthly Social Security check. You're not required to have Social Security withhold federal taxes from your monthly check, but it's often easier than making quarterly estimated tax payments.

Your financial advisor may help you reduce your overall income, or change the income sources to a more tax-friendly account, to reduce the amount of tax on benefits.

SPOUSAL/DIVORCE BENEFITS

There is another benefit you may not know about called the spousal benefit. If you are married to someone who qualifies for Social Security retirement benefits, you can claim up to fifty percent of his or her benefit. This is in addition to the full benefit your spouse claims. You are eligible for spousal benefits if you are at least age sixty-two, if you have been married for at least one year, and if your spouse already is receiving Social Security benefits.

Spousal benefits total between 32.5 percent and fifty percent of your spouse's full retirement-age benefit amount, depending on how old you are when you claim them.[13] To get the full fifty percent, you both must be at your full retirement age.

Even if you qualify for Social Security benefits on your own, you want to claim spousal benefits if taking half of your spouse's benefit is more than what you would qualify for on your own. You should take the higher of the two amounts.

If you are divorced, even if you remarried and divorced again, you can claim spousal benefits on your ex-spouse's Social Security benefit. To qualify, you must be at least age sixty-two and currently unmarried. Further, you must have been married to your ex-spouse for more than ten years, and you must not have a Social Security benefit that's more than half of your former spouse's benefit. An unmarried divorced spouse does not have to wait until the ex-spouse files for benefits if the divorce happened at least two years ago.

> "Spousal benefits often are a nice financial boost of retirement income."

Spousal benefits often are a nice financial boost of retirement income for spouses who didn't work long enough to have the required forty credits or were not high wage earners. Taking a spousal benefit does not lower the amount your spouse receives, or affect his or her Social Security benefit in any way. You are leaving money on the table if you don't take spousal benefits.

THE POSSIBILITY OF SOCIAL SECURITY RUNNING OUT OF MONEY

Many people within fifteen years of retirement have heard that Social Security is running out of money. We have known since the mid-1980s that the Social Security Trust Fund was scheduled to run out of money – and, frustratingly, our politicians have yet to do anything about it. As of January 2021, the trust fund is projected to run out of money in 2035.[14]

If nothing is done and the trust fund account actually does run out of money, Social Security will only be able to pay benefits from the amount it receives through payroll taxes. If this happens, it is expected that Social Security benefits would be reduced by twenty to twenty-five percent.

It is difficult to predict Social Security's long-term future. But given its projected financial shortfalls, our government's budget deficits, and ever-growing national debt, it's safe to say Social Security will be overhauled at some point in the not-too-distant future.

KEY TAKEAWAYS

It's your money.

The Social Security retirement benefits you qualify for are *your* money the government took from *your* paycheck for *your* retirement, so take as much as you can.

Calculate what each claiming strategy looks like for you.

With your family history in mind, look closely at the different options for taking benefits mentioned in this chapter. Talk with at least two different people who pursued each option and see if you can learn from their experience.

Be tax aware.

Talk with your tax preparer about how much you would be penalized for working while taking Social Security benefits. Also, consult your tax preparer about the amount of taxes that should be withheld from your monthly check.

Apply for benefits two months before you need them.

Once you've decided the most opportune time to start receiving benefits, apply for benefits at least two months in advance.

What to take to your meeting with Social Security.

Apply in person if possible. Take your Social Security card, birth certificate, marriage certificate if signing up for spousal benefits, divorce papers if signing up for spousal benefits from an ex-spouse, and W-2 forms or tax returns for the last two years if you are self-employed.

When you call to set the appointment, ask if you need to bring anything else so you aren't surprised. Remember, the eligibility rules and methods for calculating benefits change from time to time. Check ssa.gov to keep track of changes and how they affect your situation.

QUESTIONS FOR PERSONAL OR GROUP STUDY

1. When was the last time you checked your account with the Social Security Administration to see if your recorded "quarters" are correct?
2. What is your full retirement age (FRA)? How does that correlate with your planned retirement date?
3. Which claiming strategy did your parents take? Which strategy fits your retirement plan?
4. Do you qualify for spousal benefits? If so, when should you claim these benefits to maximize your lifetime income?

CHAPTER FOUR
INCOME

"I'm scared because I have gotten paid every two weeks for over thirty years, and starting next month, I won't anymore."

Tom had just figured out a significant change was coming, and he needed my help to prepare for it. He had enough money in his checking account, and he had a sizeable retirement account, but he didn't know how to make his retirement savings feel like his paycheck.

Retirement is great, but it does change a few things. For example, your financial focus shifts from saving money to withdrawing money. This is a significant mindset shift that feels a little scary for the first year. Now, instead of trying to be a good saver, you need to make your savings provide for you.

To do this, you need to create a steady income from your savings while at the same time protecting as much of the original balance as possible. More to the point, you are trying to keep living your normal lifestyle without running out of money or having to go back to work.

To get there, we need to look at a few areas more closely:

- How to pay yourself
- The advantages of an IRA rollover
- Two types of withdrawals
- Different withdrawal rates that help you figure out the appropriate amount for you
- Which account types to withdraw from first

PAYING YOURSELF

The phrase, "Show me the money!" from the popular 1996 movie *Jerry Maguire* is one of the most famous movie quotes of all time.[1] I think it became so celebrated because we all can relate to it, especially when we start preparing for retirement and are a little nervous about income. Many retirees just want to shout, "Please, someone show me where the money comes from!"

Many of us have worked for years. We're familiar with receiving two paychecks each month from the same place. What can make the first few months of retirement feel strange is that, most likely, you get multiple checks from several different places, and each check only arrives once a month.

For most Americans, retirement income comes from government benefits such as Social Security, a retirement account, personal savings, an inheritance, and, for some, a company pension plan. It can be tricky managing income from multiple sources, but your financial advisor can help you organize your income stream.

Some retirees are still lucky enough to have a company pension plan. If you have a pension plan where you work, or where you worked in the past, you need to consult a financial advisor to see how the different payout options fit within your retirement goals. Pay special attention to the pension options for your spouse, and ask your advisor about adding a "period certain" in case something happens to you early in retirement. "Period certain" is an annuity option that guarantees payments for a specific number of years, as opposed to the annuitant's lifetime.

Most Americans do not have a company pension plan. Rather, they've been investing in retirement through their company's retirement plan. As you approach retirement, you now need to convert your pension and/or retirement savings into a source of income.

In Chapter 2, we discussed how much of your current monthly expenses you might need when you retire. If you skipped that exercise in Chapter 2, please go back and complete it now. You want accurate information as you face retirement. For discussion in this chapter, I am using monthly expense generalities in case you're reading this before you do the number crunching.

Most of my clients need between seventy and ninety percent of their current monthly salary in retirement to maintain their lifestyles. Some retirees tell me they plan to live on less than seventy percent, but in reality, only a handful actually do. Some clients even need more in retirement than they're making now because they want to upgrade their lifestyle or move to a warmer climate.

The reason I'm using the eighty percent salary replacement example here, instead of one hundred percent, is that retirees no longer contribute to a 401(k) plan, and most likely their mortgage is paid off. In the last year of your career, if you're living off your entire salary, then you probably need closer to ninety percent of your current salary in retirement.

Here's a good rule of thumb: the higher your working salary, the smaller the replacement percentage. This is primarily because you will enter a lower tax bracket in retirement without your high salary. On average, people who make $50,000 to $70,000 a year can live on seventy percent of that in retirement, but those who earn less than $30,000 a year need more than eighty percent of their income in retirement. Now that you know about how much money you need for monthly expenses in retirement, let's look at those different income streams.

We begin with Social Security and/or pension income. Use the information from Chapter 3 to calculate your monthly Social Security benefit. If you have a pension, work with your financial advisor to determine the best payout option for you. These two monthly dollar amounts are important because your Social Security income and pension income are the starting points for total retirement income.

With your monthly Social Security and pension payment numbers in hand, calculating how much additional monthly income you need from your retirement savings is a simple matter of subtraction. Subtract the total of your retirement monthly expenses from your combined Social Security and pension payments.

As an example, let's look at Tom and Karen, who are about to retire and who make a combined $7,500 in gross monthly income (which equates to a $90,000 annual salary). In addition, Tom has a $500 monthly pension. Assuming they need eighty percent of their current income to maintain their lifestyle in retirement, Tom and Karen need approximately $6,000 in monthly retirement income.

By subtracting the $3,000 Social Security payment (estimated $1500 for each person), as well as Tom's $500 monthly pension payment, we see they are short $2,500 in income for what they need to live on in retirement. So, they need to take an additional $2,500 from their retirement savings each month to cover their expected monthly retirement expenses.

Example with Tom and Karen:

		Income/Need Calculation (Example)	
1		$7,500	Combined monthly working salary
2	×	.80	Replacement value
3		$6,000	Retirement income needed
4	−	$3,000	Less Tom and Karen's Social Security benefits
5	−	$500	Less Tom's pension payment
6		$2,500	Additional retirement income needed

These are merely estimates for the purpose of illustration. Your monthly income needs may look significantly different, but the formula remains the same.

Now, you try it. Use the form below. On line one, write down the total current monthly gross income for you and your spouse. On line two, multiply that amount by eighty percent – or whatever percentage best fits your replacement value. On line three, enter the result to get your retirement income needed. On line four, subtract the combined monthly Social Security benefits. On line five, subtract any monthly pension amount. The bottom line (line 6) should give you a good idea of the additional monthly retirement income you need.

		Income/Need Calculation Form	
1			Total current monthly gross income
2	×		Replacement value (70%, 80%, 90%)
3			Retirement income needed
4	−		Less combined Social Security benefits
5	−		Less pension payment (if applicable)
6			Additional retirement income needed

Is line six greater than zero? If so, you need additional income in retirement. That means you'll need to withdraw from your retirement savings each month to cover your living expenses. But don't fret. This is normal. Most people can't make it on Social Security and/or pensions alone.

Now that you've calculated the additional retirement income needed, let's take the next step. Using that additional retirement income figure, you can determine how to withdraw that amount from retirement savings – and estimate how long it will last. You're on the right track to getting real answers about retirement income. And that should offer you peace of mind about the entire process.

IRA ROLLOVER

Now that you know how much income you need from your retirement savings, we can focus on the advantages of an IRA rollover. Remember, retirement is not a finish line but a starting line to a new season in life. You're not finished investing just because you stop contributing to your retirement savings. You need to keep faithfully investing your retirement savings even during your retirement years. And you have two options: your old 401(k) or an IRA.

The first option is to leave your retirement savings in your employer-provided retirement plan 401(k) and continue to invest in funds the plan makes available. Many employer-provided retirement plans allow you to leave your retirement savings in their plan throughout retirement. These types of plans generally have eight to twenty investment options, which the human resources department may monitor.

The second option is to move your retirement savings into an IRA (Individual Retirement Account) at a bank or investment firm. Moving, or rolling, your retirement savings to an IRA is the most popular choice for many retirees.

There are many reasons for the popularity of this choice. Let's consider a few:

Consolidation. An IRA allows you to consolidate or combine several retirement plans you might have had from previous employers. Consolidating makes it easier to manage investments and keep track of your money.

More investment options. Generally, IRAs offer more investment options than 401(k) plans. Your employer's 401(k) might offer only twenty investment options. Meanwhile, your IRA has access to the New York Stock

Exchange, which features three thousand stocks, nearly ten thousand mutual funds, and access to countless other investment options.

Communication. A good financial advisor usually provides better communication than your former human resources department. If you leave your retirement savings with your former employer, you might at times feel like an outsider. Your former employer's focus is understandably on current employees, not former ones. The HR folks won't make you feel this way intentionally, but often former employees are "out of sight, out of mind."

Easier access. An IRA provides you with easier access to your money. With an IRA, you simply call your financial advisor's office when you want to make a change instead of having to go through the human resources department at your former employer.

Fewer rules. An IRA also has fewer IRS rules. If you leave your retirement savings with your former employer, the IRS requires the company to hold out twenty percent in federal taxes from every distribution you take from a 401(k). However, with a distribution from an IRA, you can choose to hold out the amount of tax you actually owe, or none at all if you prefer to pay taxes at the end of the year. Though I think it's best to have some taxes withheld each month, it's nice to have options and maintain control.

Continual tax deferral. If you move your tax-deferred 401(k) from your employer to a traditional IRA by an indirect rollover or direct rollover, your retirement savings continue to grow tax-deferred and allow you to delay paying income taxes until you start receiving distributions. You still pay income taxes a little at a time on each withdrawal, but you don't have to pay it all at once, and your money continues to grow on a tax-deferred basis.

Potential estate planning benefits. Your 401(k) may limit how retirement savings are paid to beneficiaries in the event of your death. So, it's wise to investigate the options available to beneficiaries so as not to unintentionally cause them tax complications. There are rules to inheriting IRAs, too. But IRAs give beneficiaries the option to take the money out over ten years, allowing them to stretch the tax-deferred savings and pay taxes a little at a time.

Since you continue investing throughout your retirement years, it's best to choose an option that gives you the greatest flexibility and opportunities. For most of you, that means rolling your retirement investments into an IRA and hiring a professional to help manage them. If you choose the IRA route, you need to open the account before you retire. That way, your employer can more easily make the transfer.

TYPES OF WITHDRAWALS

Now, let us look at two ways to access your retirement savings. One way is a so-called lump-sum distribution – withdrawing it all at once. The other way is to receive smaller, regular checks for the rest of your life. The option you choose depends on your unique situation: your age, financial situation, current financial needs, and, lastly, your current and future tax brackets.

Before we dive into the specifics of the two options, you need to remember that any pretax withdrawal you take before age fifty-nine and a half most likely means a ten percent federal income tax penalty. That's because withdrawals (distributions) from pretax retirement 401(k) plans generally are taxed as ordinary income. That means you would have to pay your normal federal and state taxes on your money, plus a ten percent penalty for early withdrawal. There are a few exceptions, like the 72(t) or an IRS-approved crisis,[2] but for the most part, you need to wait to withdraw any money from a pretax retirement account until you reach the age of fifty-nine and a half.

As I mentioned earlier, there are two ways to withdraw your money. First, there is a *single lump-sum payment* option, in which your employer sends you a check for the total of your retirement savings. This option generally is the most expensive because it forces you to pay all the income taxes due in the same tax year. A handful of retirees choose this option because they want to pay off their mortgages or cover some type of unusual expense like a medical bill.

If you choose the lump-sum option, the government forces your former employer to hold out twenty percent for federal taxes, regardless of your tax bracket. As an example, if your retirement savings was $300,000 and you requested the lump-sum payment option, you would only receive $240,000 because of the twenty percent mandatory withholding law for federal taxes.

You also should know that you might owe more than twenty percent because this option stacks your lump-sum payment on top of your regular taxable income. You just might get bumped up to really high federal and state tax brackets. That being said, I strongly suggest you consult your tax preparer before choosing this option.

The second option is a *systematic withdrawal plan*. You leave your retirement savings invested but withdraw checks over your lifetime as needed for living expenses. While most retirees withdraw one check per month to cover bills, these withdrawals can be taken quarterly, semi-annually, or annually as well.

The systematic withdrawal option gives you the flexibility to decide the dollar amount and how frequently you want your retirement income to come to you. I suggest taking systematic withdrawals as frequently as you received paychecks while working. This makes it easier to adjust.

The greatest advantage of this option is that your retirement savings remain invested while you take systematic withdrawals, helping you stay ahead of inflation. At death, the balance of your savings is payable to your beneficiaries.

Since a systematic withdrawal is the most popular, let's go a little deeper into how it could work. There are three different ways to set up your income using systematic withdrawals:

(1) *A set dollar amount on a scheduled day of each month.* For example, you might instruct your financial advisor to send you $1,500 on the first day of each month.

(2) *Dividing the total amount of your retirement savings into equal payments over a certain period of time.* Generally, this is accomplished with an annuity contract that comes with some restrictions. If you choose the annuity route, read the fine print carefully and pay close attention to fees, withdrawal penalties, and flexibility options.

(3) *Taking a certain percentage of your retirement savings out of your brokerage account on a scheduled day each month.* This is the most popular option. This is where you direct your financial advisor to pay you, for example, four percent of your total balance, divided by twelve months. Later in this chapter, I will address which percentages give you the greatest chance of success in maintaining your retirement savings.

I recommend that my clients use systematic withdrawal, with the percentage option, on a monthly basis. I believe this gives people more control of their account balance, which helps them maintain their lifestyles *and* keep up with inflation by remaining invested. Flexibility is crucial to your financial plan. You probably need to change your payout plan at least once in retirement because it is difficult to plan for unforeseen events like illnesses or accidents.

Systematic withdrawals don't guarantee your balance lasts a lifetime. None of the withdrawal options can make that promise. If you take out more money than your retirement savings are making, then your account balance goes down. It's simple economics. If your account balance goes down enough, you may run out of money. Be wise. And if you don't have financial wisdom, hire someone who does. The goal is to have adequate income that outlives you and your spouse.

Regardless of which withdrawal plan you use, whether lump-sum or systematic, all withdrawals are going to be taxed as ordinary income. Further, they probably are going to be subject to a ten percent federal tax penalty if you take withdrawals before age fifty-nine and a half unless you meet one of the few exceptions.

Roth accounts usually are exempt because you prepaid the tax. Also, make your withdrawal plan with *Required Minimum Distributions* (RMDs) in mind. Your financial advisor usually sets up your withdrawals, so make sure you take the right amount to avoid RMD penalties.

In summary, the lump-sum option gives you immediate access to all your money, but the income-tax bill is huge. Systematic withdrawals give you income from your IRA in equal distributions over time and feel much more like a paycheck. Whichever option you choose, make sure it fits into your overall financial plan.

WHAT AMOUNT SHOULD YOU WITHDRAW?

"How are you guys doing income-wise?" I asked a retired husband and wife who were long-time clients. He looked at her, and she looked back at him. They both shrugged their shoulders. Then, he said, "I guess we're doing fine! We just keep on living normally, and we haven't bounced a check yet. We don't pay much attention to it."

That peace of mind told me we had their income just right. Their accounts were continuing to grow, and they were living the way they wanted to live.

So, how much money should you withdraw from your retirement savings? The answer depends on how long you need income in retirement. Before you create an investment plan, you must consider how long you think you'll be in retirement. You don't want to take too much out and run out of money, but you also don't want to withdraw so little that you can't afford the lifestyle you desire.

You need to locate the retirement crossroad where the income you want and the withdrawal rate you need intersect. This helps ensure that you don't run out of money. Further, it helps guarantee you can chase your dreams. To help you find that crossroad, I'll show you different withdrawal rates to help you calculate just the right amount of withdrawal.

Every driver has a different approach to keeping his or her tank full. The ultraconservative driver stops at the next gas station as soon as the gas gauge crosses the half-full line. The risk taker loves the thrill of seeing just how far the needle can descend past the E before his or her vehicle sputters for lack of fuel; this driver loves coasting into the pump on fumes just for the thrill of it.

When I was a young driver, my car ran out of gas forty feet from the gas pump, and my buddy and I had to push a two-ton 1976 Monte Carlo up a slight hill to refill it. I remember thinking, "I will never let my car run out of gas again." And I haven't.

Taking money out of your retirement savings is similar to drawing down the gas in your car. You want to go where you want to go, but the last thing you want is to run out of gas. (By the way, our family, including teen drivers, has a quarter-tank rule. When the gas gauge hits the quarter mark, we stop and fill the tank before going home. Our rationale is that we never know what emergency might arise that requires quick response and ample gas in the tank.) That's a good plan for your retirement withdrawals as well. Take out as much as you need, but not so much that you can't handle an emergency if one arises.

The most popular withdrawal plan is based on a certain percentage of your total retirement savings. Here's an example: If you have a retirement balance of one million dollars and select a four percent withdrawal rate, you'll receive forty thousand dollars in annual income. Most retirees prefer a monthly distribution, so it comes out to $3,333 from your retirement savings each month to supplement your Social Security and/or pension benefits.

Here is how it breaks down:

Percentage Withdrawal Example		
	$1,000,000	Total account balance
×	0.04	Percentage multiplier (4%)
	$40,000	Annual income
÷	12	Calendar months
	$3,333	Monthly income

Now that you understand how it works, let's look at the best percentage for you in order to safely withdraw income without outliving your money. In my practice, I see many different withdrawal percentages used by my clients' former advisors – some as high as seven percent, which is just too high.

In his excellent article entitled, "Determining Withdrawal Rates Using Historical Data," William Bengen found that no more than four percent should be used as a withdrawal rate. He came to this conclusion after analyzing many different scenarios for withdrawal percentages in different market conditions. Bengen discovered that "in no case has it (4% withdrawal rate) caused a portfolio to be exhausted (run out of money) before 33 years, and in most cases, it will lead to a portfolio (lasting) 50 years or longer."[3]

Bengen's analysis assumed retirement savings were invested fifty percent in stocks and fifty percent in fixed income, frequently rebalanced so as to maintain that balance. An investment portfolio like this could possibly produce an average return of four to five percent.[4] This rate of return is based on the historical market performance of an illustrative portfolio, which cannot be guaranteed.

The benefit of a four-percent withdrawal strategy is that it gives you a reliable income that may be adjusted upward later in retirement if needed as the cost of living increases with inflation. Bengen went on to say that starting retirement at a five-percent withdrawal rate is risky; six percent or more is "gambling."[5]

You can see just how true this is in the hypothetical portfolio on the next page. This portfolio, with $500,000 in retirement savings, invested fifty percent in stocks and fifty percent in bonds, shows how the account would have performed over a thirty-year period with different withdrawal rates. The chart begins on the left-hand side in 1999, just two years before the 9/11 terror attacks in the U.S. and the negative market years that followed. It illustrates how a retiree's account would have fared during that market with withdrawal rates of four, five, six, seven, and eight percent, adjusted for inflation.[6]

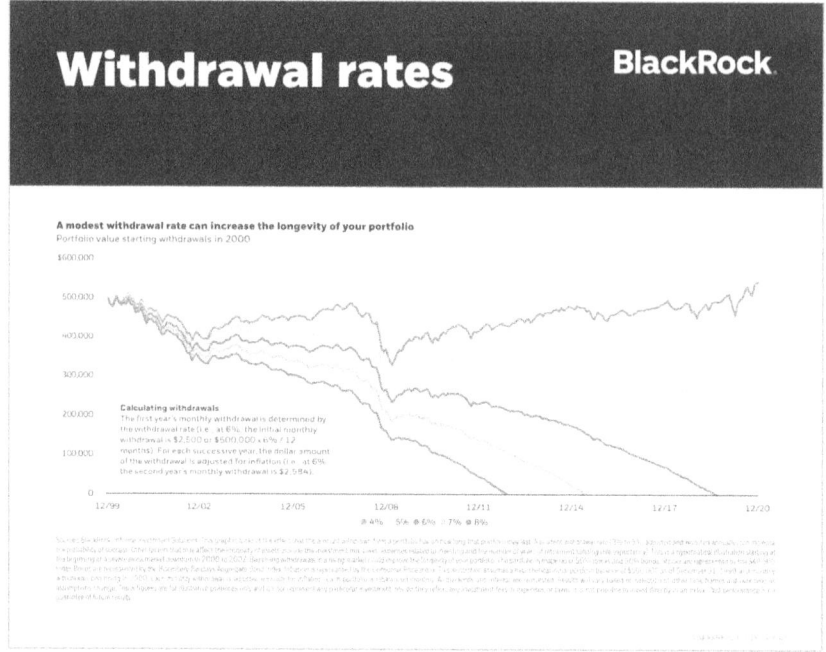

Withdrawal rate chart created by BlackRock, used by permission. Download a printable version via highstreet.press/retire.

We have no idea what the stock market will do over the next thirty years, but we're fairly certain it will have good years and bad years. Using a lower withdrawal percentage gives you peace of mind and helps your retirement savings survive as long as you do.

Let's go back to the analogy of the gas gauge in your car. Just as refueling when your car hits a quarter of a tank enables you to use your time wisely and prepare for possible emergencies, a four or five percent withdrawal rate gives you good retirement income – and it leaves wiggle room to handle unexpected crises that might arise.

FROM WHICH ACCOUNT DO YOU WITHDRAW FIRST?

Now that you know how much to withdraw from your retirement savings, we need to focus on which account types you should withdraw from first. That's not an easy decision because there are so many different types of accounts. You might be invested in taxable (nonretirement) accounts, tax-deferred (retirement or annuity) accounts, and tax-free (Roth retirement) accounts. I'll offer some general guidelines below, but consult your tax advisor to see which option works best for you.

I suggest that you spend down nonretirement accounts first. For most retirees, it makes sense to start your systematic withdrawal from nonretirement accounts. However, continue to leave six months of income in your emergency fund. These accounts are usually regular taxable brokerage accounts, certificates of deposit, bank savings accounts, individual stocks, bonds, mutual funds, or exchange-traded funds (ETFs).

I suggest you spend this money first so your tax-deferred accounts can keep growing in a tax-advantaged way until you have to start taking Required Minimum Distributions (RMDs) at age seventy-two. If possible, within these accounts, spend the investments first that have the highest cost basis. Not to get too technical, but the investments with the greatest gains (appreciated investments) have the highest capital gains tax.

Second, spend down your tax-deferred accounts. Usually, these are IRAs, employer-provided retirement plans like a 401(k), and annuities. You have to pay ordinary income tax on any withdrawals from tax-deferred investments because you invested in them before you paid taxes on them.

Of course, any withdrawals before age fifty-nine and a half incur a ten-percent income-tax penalty in addition to ordinary income taxes. At age seventy-two, the IRS forces you to begin taking income from these accounts in what is called a Required Minimum Distribution (RMD) from any traditional IRA (pretax) and 401(k) or other employer-provided retirement plan. The exact amount is calculated using IRS tables. Your financial advisor can help you avoid an IRS tax penalty of fifty percent on any amount you didn't take that you were supposed to take.

Last, spend down your tax-exempt investments. Normally, these are after-tax retirement accounts such as Roth IRAs or Roth 401(k)s. I usually suggest that my clients leave their Roth accounts for last because there's no RMD rule. You've already paid taxes on your Roth contributions, and gains on those investments are tax-free.

One Roth rule to remember is that these withdrawals must come from a Roth account that is at least five years old. Or, if it is transferred from an employer retirement plan to a Roth IRA, then the withdrawal must be at least five years from the time it was invested. So, as far as the IRS is concerned, these withdrawals are tax-free and will not affect your gross taxable income.

These are general guidelines. Your individual circumstances may demand a different withdrawal strategy, so involve your financial advisor and tax advisor in the decision-making process.

KEY TAKEAWAYS

You are now the payroll person.

Start to pay yourself income out of your retirement savings. It's both exciting and a little scary. There are lots of options for how much to take out and how to go about withdrawing your money. I suggest you make a plan with as much flexibility as possible. That way, you and your financial advisor have room to adjust as your situation changes over time.

There are two types of withdrawals.

There are two ways to withdraw retirement savings from your retirement plan. The lump-sum option is a single check, but it comes with a big income-tax bill. The most common option is a systematic withdrawal plan. You leave your retirement savings invested but withdraw checks over your lifetime as needed for living expenses. While most retirees withdraw one check per month to cover bills, these withdrawals can be taken quarterly, semi-annually, or annually as well.

Think hard about which withdrawal percentage is best for you.

You need to locate the retirement crossroad where the income you want and the withdrawal rate you need intersect. This helps ensure that you don't run out of money. Further, it helps guarantee you can chase your dreams. Make your decision slowly. I remember what my grandpa, Poppy, would say while we were sawing a board, "Measure twice, cut once." It was not original to him, but the truth connects. Either way, take your time making these decisions, and give yourself as much flexibility as possible.

Have a plan for which account you withdraw from first.

Make a list of your investments, such as taxable (non-retirement) accounts, tax-deferred (retirement or annuity) accounts, and tax-free (Roth retirement) accounts. Figure out the accounts from which you should take retirement income withdrawals first. That helps you avoid the most taxes and enables your accounts to grow. You can do this.

QUESTIONS FOR PERSONAL OR GROUP STUDY

1. What is your monthly income shortfall? Do you have any other income sources that could narrow the gap?
2. How are you currently paid: monthly, weekly, or quarterly? What frequency works best for you in retirement so that your income stream matches the cycle of bills you receive?
3. What withdrawal percentage makes you the most comfortable? Consider your current financial situation and your longevity.
4. List your various retirement income sources. Do you expect any other sources of income, such as an inheritance?

CHAPTER FIVE
INVESTMENT TOOLS

Her husband said, "Why are we even having this meeting?"

I manage the retirement plans for several large companies and universities. Often, I encourage employees to bring their spouses to our last meeting before they retire. In this case, the employee's husband had to take off work to attend the meeting and concluded it was a huge waste of time. His rationale: "She had made it to retirement and was finished with investing."

Then, I asked, "So what is your plan for these investments the day after you both retire?"

Awkward silence.

Retirement is not a finish line. Often, when you think about your retirement accounts, you're just hoping not to mess things up, or lose it all in the final month. Some people act as if they're running an obstacle course while holding a glass of water. They're so afraid of spilling it, they can't wait to set the glass down on the finish line. Maybe you live in constant fear that the market will crash *just before* you retire. Or, maybe you can't wait to retire so you just don't have to worry about it anymore.

You need to ditch that mentality! Retirement is not a finish line. You're not "safe" because you've stopped working. Rather, retirement is the starting line for a new kind of investing season in your life. It is a season that spans days, months, and years. This new season needs a good investment plan that matches your risk tolerance and length of time you plan to live off the fruits of these investments.

When you were investing in your company's retirement plan, you may have felt alone, constantly worried you were making mistakes. Having both a good investment plan and a trustworthy advisor help reduce some of the worries you may have about making the "right" decisions for your money. Your retirement account needs to remain invested so it continues to grow.

> "Retirement is the starting line for a new kind of investing season in your life."

That being said, now might be a good time to reevaluate the risk level you desire for your retirement investments. Remember: this is a change in mindset. Instead of putting money *into* retirement savings accounts, you're taking money *out*.

When approaching retirement investments, you need to consider:

- How to flip the switch in your mind from *saving* for retirement to *withdrawing* savings for retirement income.
- Why combining multiple investment accounts makes it easier for you to keep track of them.
- How to keep your investment risk in line with asset allocations.
- And how an Investor Risk Profile Questionnaire helps you learn how much risk you're comfortable with.

FLIPPING THE SWITCH FROM SAVING TO WITHDRAWING

Up to this point, your investment goal has been to grow your retirement account. But when you stop working full-time, the focus on your finances changes, and so does your investment strategy. Before you retire, the number one goal for your investments is to grow the account as fast as possible. You still want your investments to grow in retirement. However, after you retire, receiving income from your investment account becomes the main goal, and growing the account becomes the secondary goal.

The reason income becomes the main goal after retirement is because you're taking money out of your retirement account (distributions) and living off that income as a replacement for your paycheck. To do this effectively, you might need to change (reallocate) your investments so that a larger portion is in lower-risk investments. This lessens the chance that a market crash permanently hurts your account. If you're invested too aggressively, a severe market drop in the early years of retirement could be disastrous to your retirement plans.

If you're relying on investments to replace some or all of your work income in your retirement, it's wise to lower your investment risk to soften the blow of a potential market drop. The types of investments you're looking for are more predictable and are dividend-yield focused. Just like a farmer buys a field and sows seed looking for yield, you need investments that give you predictable monthly income. Reliable and predictable income is your new investment friend.

Put a written investment plan in place. Then, relax and watch it work. After you've hired a trustworthy advisor and developed a retirement plan, let the advisor focus on the daily ups and downs of the market. Many of my clients tell me they used to watch the news every night and cringe when the market dropped. But now, because they have both a good advisor and a solid plan, they don't worry about it anymore.

> "Reliable and predictable income is your new investment friend."

By hiring a trustworthy professional and having a good investment plan, you're able to focus on the long-term goals and successfully flip the switch from *saving* for retirement to *withdrawing* from your retirement accounts.

COMBINE YOUR INVESTMENT ACCOUNTS

My dad worked on small engines in his spare time for extra money, and often I helped him. I remember when we would tear down a motor and lay out the parts, my dad always reminded me of the KISS principle: "Keep it simple, Stupid." Like most other things in life, keeping things simple and in order makes them easier to manage. This is true when it comes to having multiple retirement plans, too.

Many people work for several different companies during their careers, and that could mean they have 401(k) retirement accounts at each of them. If this describes your situation, you would be wise to combine all of your retirement accounts into a single Individual Retirement Account (IRA). This makes it easier to organize your accounts, plan your income distribution, and track your government-mandated Required Minimum Distribution (RMD).

The most important benefit of combining these orphan accounts is that it allows you to keep control of your risk level. Having investments in multiple locations makes it difficult to monitor your overall investment risk level. Not only that, but you do yourself a favor by combining your investment accounts so that you only receive one statement each month, and you only need to call one number to get information or make a change. Combining accounts takes the pressure off you and reduces stress by eliminating some confusion.

Many people choose to roll their different work retirement accounts into an IRA. There are no tax consequences in doing this since these are going from a group retirement account to an individual retirement account. Simply put, since your retirement savings stay in a retirement account, you're not forced to pay taxes on the transfer. Your investments remain tax-sheltered in this IRA until you make withdrawals.

There are several different types of retirement accounts you can combine into your IRA. Examples include 401(k) retirement plans; 403(b) retirement plans; traditional IRAs; simple IRAs; thrift savings plans; 457(b) plans; profit-sharing plans; employee stock ownership plans (ESOPs); defined contribution plans; tax-sheltered annuities (TSA); and simplified employee pensions (SEP).

However, remember that if you withdraw funds from your traditional IRA or employer-sponsored retirement plan before age fifty-nine and six months, you could be hit with a ten percent federal tax penalty, in addition to state and federal income taxes. There are some exceptions to this penalty, but very few. Distributions are taxed as ordinary income (with annuities, only earnings are taxed). There is no ten-percent federal income-tax penalty if you take money out after you reach age fifty-nine and six months, but you still have to pay state and federal income taxes.

> "Put a written investment plan in place, and then relax and watch it work."

USING ASSET ALLOCATION TO REDUCE INVESTMENT RISK

As you approach retirement, it's up to you to make decisions about the investments in your current portfolio. Do you keep them, sell them, or simply adjust them? The answer is different for everyone, but some adjustments need to be made in order to reduce risk and set up monthly income distributions.

I tend to get the same answer when I ask people nearing retirement about their comfort level with investment risk. They say something like, "I can't lose it because I won't be making any more money." As we've already seen, this is the wrong answer. And it's the primary reason you may need to reduce your investment risk to preserve your account balance.

At times, people who've been retired for a few years, and who have managed their own accounts, hire me to fix the mess they made. Often, they were invested too aggressively or made emotional investing decisions. They bought when they should have sold, and sold when they should have bought. They watched their retirement accounts shrink when the market dropped. Many of them compounded their problems by trying to fix things by throwing good money after bad money. Doubling down on a bad investment usually doesn't work.

Out of the blue one day, a man whose investments I had managed for a few years stopped by to withdraw half of all his investments. I asked him why, and he told me he wanted to "invest it in something else, probably a CD at the bank." A little over two months later, he stopped by again and was visibly shaken. He said, "I need you to fix a mess I made."

> **"Doubling down on a bad investment usually doesn't work."**

Turns out, instead of putting half of his investments into a bank CD for safety, he did just the opposite. He put it on one stock his buddy convinced him was a sure thing. His $500,000 was now worth $10,000. He was devastated. And to make matters worse, his wife didn't know about it.

I can fix a lot of things, but there was nothing I could do about that. I reinvested the $10,000, but the $490,000 was gone for good when the stock when south. When you're retired, you simply can't take that kind of risk.

There isn't time for lost investments like that to recover, no matter how well the market may turn.

I used this illustration in my first book, *Biblical Retirement*, and it's still true:

> Think of it like this: You "down-shift" a standard transmission from fifth to fourth to third gear when coming to a stop sign or going down a steep hill. In the same way, people should lower the risk level of their investments the closer they get to an employment stop.[1]

In retirement, most people should take income distributions while their investments still earn enough to keep the account balance relatively stable. If your retirement account drops significantly near the date you planned to retire, you either have to settle for lower retirement income payments or delay retirement for a few years so you can give your account time to recover from the market drop.[2]

Maintaining a healthy risk level is incredibly important. When you were younger, you could be more aggressive because you had time to wait for the market to recover if your account went down. But when you're close to retirement, or are already retired, you have to be more cautious.

Remember, the more you chase high returns, the greater the risk you take with your retirement nest egg. The time to aggressively grow a retirement account is when you are still working and contributing money each month, *not* in retirement when you can't recover from a loss.

The stock market is extremely unpredictable. Financial markets change unexpectedly and, at times, dramatically. One way to manage your risk is to have a good *asset allocation*. An asset allocation is an investment strategy that tries to balance risk and reward by spreading a portfolio's investments out according to the investor's goals, risk tolerance, and investment horizon.[3] Often, an asset allocation strategically invests in three different asset classes: stocks (equities), bonds (fixed-income), and cash alternatives to potentially seek out the highest return within your risk tolerance.[4]

Asset allocation is a type of sophisticated investing that uses statistical analysis to manage how the three different asset classes work together in a portfolio. Asset allocation considers your investment objectives, time frame, and risk tolerance to help regulate/stabilize your portfolio for a potentially better rate of return. Asset allocation *doesn't* guarantee a profit or protect you against investment loss, but it's a time-tested method to help manage investment risk. In simple terms, this type of investing gives you a better chance of success.

Rarely in investing is there a "set it and forget it" method, and an asset allocation portfolio isn't, either. You or your advisor need to keep your investment allocations on track. All portfolios drift out of the investment alignment over time, especially when there's a lot of market movement and different parts of the portfolio outperform others.

> "Maintaining a healthy risk level is incredibly important."

In an up market, your portfolio might get over-weighted towards equities, which could unintentionally raise your investment risk. For instance, a 60/40 allocation (sixty percent equities and forty percent fixed income) might become weighted 74/26 in a good year.

> "An asset allocation gives you a better chance of success."

In the same way, in a year in which stocks perform poorly and fixed income or bonds do well, the fixed-income investment could cause your portfolio to drift the other way. This could unintentionally make your portfolio too conservative to reach your long-term investment goals. For instance, a 60/40 allocation (sixty percent equities and forty percent fixed income) might become weighted 45/55 in a year when bonds outperform stocks. Every investor should occasionally review investment allocations.

EXAMPLES OF DIFFERENT ASSET ALLOCATIONS

Below are three sample risk-based asset-allocation categories. They are hypothetical and only for illustration. It's also wise to diversify within the asset classes. For example, your equities could be diversified into growth, value, or blend, and even more so by diversifying into large-, mid-, and small-cap companies as well as domestic and international stocks.[5] These three models only show the splits between main categories, not subcategories.

Example one: conservative asset allocation – A conservative investor might have an allocation such as twenty-five percent in stocks (equities) and seventy-five percent in bonds/cash (fixed income). This allocation mix is for a retiree who doesn't like a lot of investment risk and whose investment goal is to protect the account balance while producing income.

Example two: moderate asset allocation – A moderate risk investor might have an allocation such as sixty percent in stocks (equities) and forty percent in bonds/cash (fixed income). This allocation mix is for a retiree whose investment goal is income with some investment growth, but who still wants a little cushion to protect the account balance.

Example three: aggressive asset allocation – An aggressive investor might have an allocation such as eighty-five percent in stocks (equities) and fifteen percent in bonds/cash (fixed income). This allocation mix is for a retiree who has a high tolerance for risk with a long-time frame, and whose goal is to see investments grow rather than generate income. Generally, this is a retiree who doesn't need the income and plans to pass investments on to beneficiaries. Usually, this allocation is too aggressive for most retirees, but it makes a good comparison to the conservative and moderate allocations models.

These sample risk-based asset-allocation categories range from slightly volatile to very volatile. Determining which one is best for you depends on several factors, such as your total net worth, how many sources of income you have, how much debt you've incurred, your health/longevity, and how much you worry about loss in your retirement accounts.

COMPARISON OF ASSET ALLOCATION PERFORMANCES

Now, let's look at how these three allocation portfolios would perform over a hypothetical twenty-year period of time. The first portfolio features a *conservative allocation* that has twenty-five percent of its assets in stocks and seventy-five percent in bonds/cash. The second portfolio shows a *moderate allocation* that has sixty percent of its assets in stocks and forty percent in bonds/cash. The third portfolio illustrates an *aggressive allocation* that has eighty-five percent of its assets in stocks and fifteen percent in bonds/cash.

From January 1, 2000 to December 31, 2020, the hypothetical *aggressive* portfolio was quite volatile, with several peaks and valleys including the financial crisis of 2007-2008 and the pandemic in 2020. Over the twenty years, in its best twelve months, the aggressive portfolio returned 47.64

percent (March 2009 – February 2010); in its worst twelve months, it lost 38.38 percent (March 2008 – February 2009). Overall, the *aggressive* portfolio averaged a 6.85 percent annual rate of return over twenty years.

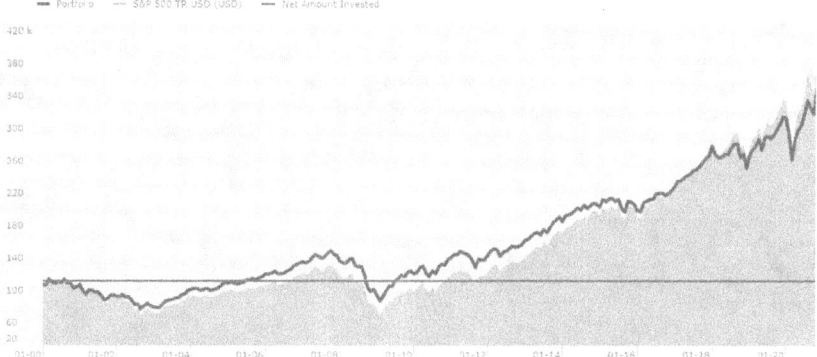

During the same twenty-year period, the hypothetical *moderate* portfolio was somewhat more balanced. It, too, showed peaks and valleys, including the financial crisis of 2007-2008 and the pandemic of 2020. But overall, this portfolio was less volatile than the aggressive portfolio. Over the twenty years, in its best twelve months, the moderate portfolio returned 35.14 percent (March 2009 – February 2010); in its worst twelve months, it lost 27.0 percent (March 2008 – February 2009). In the end, the *moderate* portfolio averaged a 6.46 percent annual rate of return over twenty years.

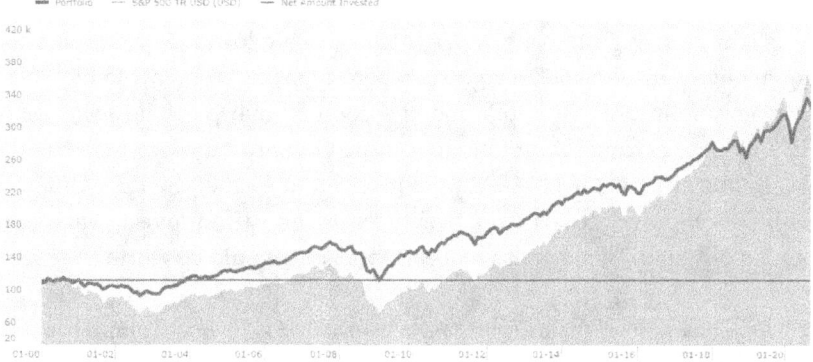

From January 1, 2000 to December 31, 2020, the hypothetical *conservative* portfolio was much less volatile – and even somewhat predictable, although it also went through the financial crisis of 2007-2008 and the pandemic of 2020. Over the twenty years, in its best twelve months, the conservative portfolio returned 19.16 percent (March 2009 – February 2010); in its worst twelve months it lost 10.20 percent (March 2008 – February 2009). Overall, the *conservative* portfolio averaged a 5.56 percent annual rate of return over twenty years.

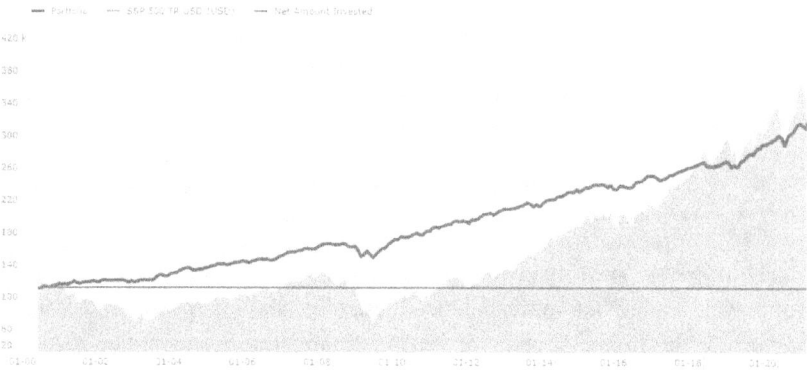

Keep in mind, all three portfolios we just reviewed are *hypothetical* examples; actual results may vary.

So, which portfolio is best? That depends on your situation. The difference between a 6.85 percent return, a 6.46 percent return and a 5.56 percent return can add up over time. The difference between the aggressive portfolio and the conservative portfolio was only about 1.3 percent, but there was a huge swing in volatility (big highs and big lows). At one point, the aggressive portfolio had an eighty-six percent swing from low to high over a twenty-four-month period, and the conservative portfolio *only* had a twenty-nine percent swing from low to high over twenty-four months.

In this example, if $100,000 were invested in each of the three different risk allocation portfolios over twenty years, and if no investments were added or withdrawn, here's what each portfolio would be worth:

- The aggressive portfolio that produced a 6.85 percent annual rate of return would be worth $376,574.
- The moderate portfolio that produced a 6.46 percent annual rate of return would be worth $349,947.

- And the conservative portfolio that produced a 5.56 percent annual rate of return would be worth $295,331.

As you can see, there's more than an $80,000 difference between the conservative and aggressive portfolios, but only about a $25,000 difference between the moderate and aggressive portfolios. The right portfolio for you is the one in which you have the most opportunity for return for the amount of risk and volatility you can stomach.

Everyone wishes they could invest where there is high income and low risk, but those investments don't exist. As mentioned earlier, inflation should be a consideration, so it might be wise to keep a portion of your portfolio in stocks to counter inflation over time. How do you determine which asset allocation is best for you? And are you wondering just how much risk tolerance you have? Find out by taking the following Investor Risk Profile Questionnaire.

> "Everyone wishes they could invest where there is high income and low risk, but those investments don't exist."

INVESTOR RISK PROFILE QUESTIONNAIRE

You need to identify your tolerance for investment risk in order to determine which asset allocation is best for you. A helpful tool is an Investor Risk Profile Questionnaire. This involves a series of questions about your investment goals and your personality. There are no wrong answers because the questionnaire follows your personal preferences, and it measures your reaction to market volatility.

The questionnaire offers a good gauge of your risk tolerance. It also suggests an asset allocation. Below is a sample Investor Risk Profile Questionnaire you may enjoy taking. It features five risk allocation models.

RISK TOLERANCE QUESTIONNAIRE

The Risk Tolerance Questionnaire helps you discover your risk comfort level for an investment portfolio. Answer the questions below as best you can. There are no wrong answers because each answer reflects your feelings toward investing. Place the number corresponding to your answer in the box to the right.

➤ **Time Horizon**

What is the time frame to achieve your goals?
5. 15 years or longer   **4.** 10-15 years   **3.** 5-10 years   **2.** 1-5 years   **1.** Immediately

What is your age?
5. 45 or under   **4.** 46-55   **3.** 56-65   **2.** 66-75   **1.** 76 or over

➤ **Financial Goals**

Which statement below best describes your goal for this investment?
5. Aggressively grow my account over a short time frame
4. Grow my account significantly over a long period
3. Create current income and grow the assets over a longer time frame
2. Generate high current income
1. Preserve the balance and create some income

In five years, what do you expect your portfolio balance to be?
5. Significantly greater than it is today
4. Greater than it is today
3. Somewhat more than it is today
2. Slightly more than today
1. I'm more concerned about my current income

➤ **Risk Tolerance**

If your portfolio suddenly declined by 15% which one of these statements would express your feelings?
5. I invest for long-term growth and can accept short-term fluctuations.
4. I invest for long-term growth, but a temporary decline would concern me.
3. It wouldn't bother me if my income was unaffected.
2. I'd be concerned.
1. I'd be very concerned; I want to avoid any potential loss.

Which of the following investments would you feel most comfortable owning?
5. Stocks in small growth companies
4. Stocks in midsize growth companies
3. Stocks in older, large, established companies
2. US Government securities
1. Certificates of deposit

How optimistic are you about the economy in the long term?
5. Very optimistic   **4.** Somewhat optimistic   **3.** Unsure   **2.** Pessimistic   **1.** Very pessimistic

* Total your score in the bottom right-hand box.
Match your score to the legend on the next page.   **Total Score

Download a printable version via highstreet.press/retire.

Your investor profile is based on your combined responses, with no single question as the determining factor. Typically, a participant answers all the questions, totals the answers, and compares the total score to the corresponding asset allocation on the left.

Match your total score with one of the investment objectives listed below. If your score is near the top or bottom of a total range, you may want to examine the next or previous category to see which one sounds more like you.

As a note, an increased score also increases risk, volatility, and investment return expectations.

Conservative Allocation **Score 7-15**
- Need for capital preservation with a secondary goal for current income
- The asset mix has a higher concentration for fixed income and a lesser concentration on equities
- Lowest tolerance for risk and shortest investment horizon

Moderate Allocation **Score 16-29**
- Focused on growth and current income
- The asset mix is closer to being balanced between equities and fixed income investments
- Moderate tolerance for risk and intermediate investment horizon

Aggressive Allocation **Score 30-35**
- Focused on aggressive growth with no need for current income
- The asset mix has the highest concentration of equities
- Highest tolerance for risk and longest investment horizon

The investment objectives shown are for illustrative purposes only. Your investment objective is based on many factors, including your financial situation, tolerance for risk, time horizon, and other financial needs. Consult your financial advisor if you have any questions.

Download a printable version via highstreet.press/retire.

An Investor Risk Profile Questionnaire isn't perfect, but it's a good guide to your investment plan. It helps you direct how, why, and where your money should be invested. You should consider it a living document because it needs updating every three years or so as your goals and circumstances change.

KEY TAKEAWAYS

Invest right now.

The most important thing to remember from this chapter is that you need to invest in *something*. Financial "doers" see increases, but financial "hoarders" get nothing. Use an Investor Risk Profile Questionnaire to help guide you into the right investment allocation based on your risk tolerance. The right risk allocation helps you know *how* to invest in a way that aligns with your risk tolerance, while maintaining proper diversification to help you reach your investment goals over time and soften the effects of market downturns.

Estimate the number of years you expect to need investment income.

A vital part of your plan is determining the number of years your portfolio needs to provide you with income. A retiree's investment time frame is the number of years he or she expects to live in retirement. In most cases, the longer a person's time frame, the more important it is to put some of the portfolio into stocks. If someone has a shorter time frame – possibly because of a serious illness – he or she may want the portfolio to weigh heavily on bonds and fixed-income investments to soften the effects of market downturns.

Be prepared for market volatility.

In my practice, I see a troubling trend among retirees who visit me after they've been working with someone else. A lot of these retirees are not properly planning for the ups and downs of the market. Investment volatility happens. It's not a question of *if* but *when* it will happen. Many retirees invested too aggressively and watched their retirement accounts shrink with market loss because they took too many risks. In retirement, you are not trying to aggressively grow your investment account; rather, you should be somewhat more conservative in order to have income and preserve your balance.

Hire an expert.

Enlist a professional wealth manager to help you allocate your retirement investments. Get wise financial counsel you can trust when the markets change – as they will. In Chapter 7, I provide guidance on finding a financial advisor. A good financial advisor can offer a seasoned perspective and experience to help you achieve your financial goals. This is too important to "wing it."

QUESTIONS FOR PERSONAL OR GROUP STUDY

1. What do you need to do to start flipping the mental switch from *saving* for retirement to *withdrawing* from your retirement accounts?
2. Are there any companies you once worked for that still hold a 401(k) in your name? If so, call the human resources department at each of these organizations to confirm account balances.
3. If you do have various 401(k) accounts with former employers, what's your next step?
4. When you think about investing goals, risk tolerance, and your investment horizon, what are the main differences between how you're investing now and how you should be investing for the future?
5. Did you take the Investor Risk Profile Questionnaire? Which risk category best describes you? Which risk allocation model best suits you?

CHAPTER SIX
ESTATE PLANNING

"Finish strong!"

One of my clients called my office and scheduled an appointment. She wanted to review her beneficiaries (people who inherit her accounts when she dies). This seemed a little odd to me, since I regularly schedule such reviews with my clients. When we met, I asked if something was wrong. She said no, but she didn't want to repeat her brother's mistake.

As it turns out, her brother had recently passed without updating the beneficiary information on his retirement account. His wife of three years found out a few weeks after the funeral that her husband's ex-wife was going to receive both his retirement account and life insurance proceeds because he failed to update the beneficiaries after his divorce.

In case you're wondering, the ex-wife refused to help pay for the funeral. The new wife inherited her husband's debts and funeral expenses, but none of his assets.

When approaching retirement, it's wise to plan for all aspects of it. This includes how you want your assets distributed after you pass away.

Let's consider five key elements of asset distribution:

- Why estate planning is important to you and your beneficiaries (probate and estate taxes).
- How to designate someone to make financial and/or healthcare decisions for you.
- What legal tools are available to help you distribute your assets.

- What strategies are available to help maximize charitable giving.
- How a letter to your beneficiaries may help reduce confusion and conflict.

My daughter is a fast-pitch softball pitcher. She is a Greg Maddux-style pitcher who can make the ball do crazy things. She is good now, but there was a time when she wasn't able to finish off batters. She would get two quick strikes on an opposing player, but then it seemed as if she mentally relaxed and threw a couple of balls.

I remember hearing her coach yell from the dugout, "Finish strong!" Those words of exhortation jolted her into focus and helped her get the batter out. Now, as a veteran pitcher, she remains fixated on the batter from beginning to end. She realizes the last pitch is just as important as the first one.

In the same way, you should pay just as much attention to your beneficiaries as you do to your investments. You see, the last part of your plan is just as important as the first.

Estate planning is not just for wealthy people. Every retiree needs it, regardless of the size of their investments or how much real estate they own. Estate planning is first and foremost a customized plan to decide how your property and other possessions are distributed. It passes your investments and other assets on to your family while minimizing taxes.

> "Estate planning is not just for wealthy retirees."

I'm not an attorney, nor am I offering legal advice, but I am telling you to do some financial planning with a trusted estate-planning attorney. As you set up your financial plan for retirement, speak with an attorney who guides you through the process within the framework of current tax laws.

PROBATE AND ESTATE TAXES

Good estate planning – the planning of how assets and liabilities are disbursed after death – helps you avoid financial jail, otherwise known as probate. Probate is the court proceeding that handles a deceased person's legal and financial matters. The probate court settles any disagreements over a deceased person's estate by making sure creditors get paid. It also provides an opportunity to anyone to challenge how the assets of the deceased are distributed.

The frustrating part of probate court is that it can be slow, expensive, and very public. Probate proceedings move at a snail's pace. An estate going through probate can expect to be tied up for six months to a year – and sometimes longer for more complex estates. As for the cost, each state has different rules, but probate and administrative fees can take a huge chunk of the gross estate.

Lawyers.com conducted a survey in 2019, which found that the average attorney fee was thirty-two percent of the estate to settle that estate through probate.[1] If you're a private person by nature, then you're going to hate probate court. Since the probate proceeding is a legal process, taking place in a public court, many of the documents are open to public view.

If someone wanted to look up the details of your estate, it would be easy to do so. Information such as the value of your estate and the names of your beneficiaries is easily accessible. Someone could even obtain a copy of your will if they wished. Generally, accounts that have a beneficiary designation, such as annuities, life insurance, IRAs, and 401(k)s are excluded from probate because they are held in trusts.

As for estate taxes, legislation over the years has increased the amount of an estate that is excluded from federal estate taxes. That's good news. Since the enactment of the Tax Relief Act in 2010, the federal estate tax exclusion has been five million dollars or more. Further, the 2012 American Taxpayer Relief Act made the five million exclusion permanent with adjustments for inflation each year.

In 2021, an estate valued at less than $11.7 million ($23.4 million for some married couples) is excluded from federal estate taxes.[2] This law is set to expire after 2025, and the Biden Administration is signaling that the estate values will be lowered, which could make your estate liable for estate taxes.

Though you might have dodged federal estate taxes, there could be state estate taxes or an inheritance tax for your beneficiaries, depending on the state in which you die. As of 2021, Connecticut, Hawaii, Illinois, Maine, Maryland, Massachusetts, Minnesota, New York, Oregon, Rhode Island, Vermont, Washington, and Washington, D.C. all charge state estate taxes. If you have a large estate and live in one of these states, you could owe estate taxes at both the federal and state levels. In addition to state estate taxes, there are six states – Iowa, Kentucky, Maryland, Nebraska, New Jersey, and Pennsylvania – that levy an inheritance tax.[3]

The main difference between estate taxes and inheritance taxes is that the estate pays estate taxes, but the beneficiary pays inheritance taxes. Make a note not to die in Maryland, because if you die there, your estate and beneficiaries might have to pay federal estate tax, state estate tax, and an inheritance tax. The moral of this depressing tax story is this: manage your wealth during your lifetime so the impact of taxes on your estate is minimal.

A good estate plan has other benefits, too. First, it might reduce the chance of family conflict. When your wishes are spelled out in detail, there is less chance that someone will contest how you have chosen to distribute your estate.

Second, a good estate plan can avoid the probate delays described above since you dealt with any issues prior to your death.

Last, a good estate plan can help avoid certain legal and court expenses. There is no "silver bullet" estate plan because laws continually change. But by choosing the appropriate strategies and distribution methods during your lifetime, you may help protect your beneficiaries.

The following paragraphs provide a summary of estate-planning tools and concepts currently available to help you designate someone to make financial and/or healthcare decisions for you, distribute your assets, and maximize charitable giving. Again, I'm not offering legal advice, but I am encouraging you to think about what you need to discuss with an attorney.

DESIGNATING SOMEONE TO MAKE FINANCIAL AND/OR HEALTHCARE DECISIONS FOR YOU

Powers of attorney and living wills typically are parts of an estate plan. These tools generally allow a person you designate to make financial and/or healthcare decisions for you.

A *power of attorney (POA)* gives a trusted person the authority to make decisions on your behalf in financial and legal matters.[4] A POA may grant general authority, or it could be limited to a specific activity like closing the sale of your home. This authority to act on your behalf could be granted temporarily or permanently, and it could be given immediately or in the future, such as when you're no longer able to act for yourself due to a mental or physical disability.

A power of attorney also may be revoked, but most states require you to notify the person you named in writing. You should consider including one or more POAs as part of your estate plan. My wife and I have POAs on each other, and it allowed her to sign my name on the title of a vehicle that sold while I was out of the country.

A *medical power of attorney*, or "medical proxy," is a specific type of POA. A medical power of attorney is a revocable document that gives authority to another person to make healthcare decisions on your behalf. This authority is only activated once you experience an incapacitating medical situation, such as severe Alzheimer's disease, dementia, a vegetative state, or a coma.

A *health care directive*, or "living will," is a document that helps you dictate medical decisions before they happen. It gives medical professionals instructions concerning your care during incapacitation or end-of-life situations such as artificial life support, resuscitation, or DNR (do-not-resuscitate) instructions.

This document is more specific than the medical power of attorney and includes all healthcare situations when you cannot make those decisions for yourself. Many estate planners recommend preparing both documents as part of your overall plan. The health care directive tells the person you have authorized as your medical power of attorney what to do, and it enables you to make the hard decisions for your family members so they don't have to make the decisions on their own.

I will never forget the day I sat in a college biology class and listened to my professor describe in detail how awful it was to make end-of-life decisions for his wife, who was dying of cancer. This professor didn't share personal thoughts very often. But on this day, he was highly emotional as he explained how a health care directive worked and why we should get one.

I was so moved that even though I was only nineteen, I drove to the local hospital, picked up a free health care directive, and filled it out. I even had my college roommate sign as my witness. I didn't want my family to go through what my professor went through. I still have one and review it every few years.

One of my personal mottos is, "The

> **"The best decisions you ever have to make are the ones you don't have to make."**

best decisions you ever have to make are the ones you don't have to make." A health care directive makes the decisions ahead of time so your loved ones know your wishes.

ASSET DISTRIBUTION TOOLS

There are a few different ways to distribute your remaining assets (estate) to your beneficiaries or heirs. Each option has its pros and cons. And each option allows a different level of control over the process of dispersing your assets to people or organizations you've chosen. For simplicity, let's focus on wills and trusts because they are most frequently used.

A *will* is your written instructions detailing how and to whom your estate should be distributed. Though a will is the simplest form of estate planning, it is still a legal document, when properly prepared, signed, and witnessed. And it communicates your wishes to the courts. Usually, in a will, a person names a personal representative (executor) to settle the estate.

A will guarantees your estate goes through probate. However, it also provides the court with instructions for distributing property to your heirs. A will allows you to leave your property to anyone you choose, such as a surviving spouse, a child, a grandchild, other relatives, friends, a trust, your church, or another charity. It's also the best way to specify who gets your heirlooms.

A will: (a) enables you to specify the distribution of your assets; (b) lets you designate an executor; (c) communicates the beneficiaries to the probate court; (d) allows you to create a legal trust; and (e) provides an opportunity to reduce taxes.

A *trust* is very different from a will, though a trust has a will in it. A will expresses your wishes, whereas a trust makes your wishes happen. Trusts are active before and after your death.

There are two main types of trusts: a **testamentary trust**, which only takes effect at death, and a **living trust,** which takes effect while you're still alive.

The most popular is a living trust. Generally, when people establish living trusts, they transfer the title of all their assets (cars, boats, land, etc.) from them personally to the trust. This transfer of ownership means they no longer own these assets (because the trust they control owns them). So, when they die, the assets don't go through probate because the owner (the trust) is still "alive" and ready to distribute the assets.

Not only does a trust enable the assets held by the trust to avoid probate court, but the trust also ensures how property is divided, how much cash is invested, and how assets are to be handled. After death, the trust pays your debts, and your assets in the trust are distributed to your heirs according to your written instructions. Because the court is not involved, you maintain complete control of the distribution of your estate because you set it up beforehand.

Here's another bonus: unlike a will that becomes public information after you die, a revocable trust keeps your financial affairs private. Understand that a trust is a complicated document. It is critical for you to hire an experienced attorney who is able to guide you through the process of deciding which type of trust is most appropriate for your situation.

A trust: (a) allows you to serve as your own trustee; (b) enables you to make changes at any time; (c) makes it possible to add or remove property at any time; (d) allows you to transfer authority to a successor trustee if you're incapacitated; (e) is confidential; (f) allows you to avoid probate court; (g) makes your settlement almost immediate; and (h) gives you options to reduce taxes.

CHARITABLE ESTATE PLANNING

Many retirees consider giving some of their wealth to charity. Charitable giving is a great way for many retirees to support their church and other nonprofit organizations. Giving part of your estate to charity can help both the charity and you. Charitable giving can provide tax advantages that benefit you and your beneficiaries.

Financially speaking, charitable giving can be an important part of your estate, tax, and financial planning. There are several charitable tools available, depending on the type of estate you have, how much you want to give, and when you want to give it. Each charitable tool carries with it different gift tax, income tax, and estate tax consequences. The best tool for your situation depends on what you're trying to accomplish.

There are three basic types of charitable estate planning tools available:

- Direct gifts during your lifetime
- Direct charitable gifts upon your death
- Deferred charitable gifts during your lifetime

Direct Gifts During Your Lifetime

Direct gifts during your lifetime provide needed funding for organizations and/or ministries, and they provide a current income-tax deduction. One way of accomplishing this is by moving assets while you're still alive to a *charitable lead trust* (CLT). A charitable lead trust is a gifting strategy using an irrevocable trust, which gives money to the charities of your choice for a specific period of time. At your death, or the specified time period of up to twenty years, whichever comes first, the assets pass on to your family members or other beneficiaries.

Here's an example: Let's say you own a farm and lease out the land. You place the farm's acreage into a charitable lead trust. The rent from the lease goes to the charity you choose, but the farmland goes to your beneficiaries when the time period expires, or at your death.

This way, your favorite charity receives income payments during your lifetime, but at your death, or at the end of the specified time period, the assets and income payments go to your beneficiaries. Essentially, you are donating the income from a charitable gift while retaining ownership of it.

Direct Charitable Gifts Upon Your Death

A simple and direct way to give to a charity at your death is to name your chosen charity a beneficiary. An example of this would be naming your charity as a percentage beneficiary – say, ten percent – along with your family members on your IRA.

Another direct way is to name your charity in your will. You write a sentence in your will that states the amount or specific item you'd like to leave to the charity. Be specific, use the serial or account numbers if available, and use the legal name of the charity because some charities have similar names. An example of this would be donating your jewelry to a favorite charity upon your death.

Deferred Charitable Gifts During Your Lifetime

There are a few more options available if you want to defer gifts to a charity during your lifetime. These depend on your goals and estate size. The most popular are a *charitable gift annuity*, *charitable life insurance*, and *charitable remainder trust*.

Charitable gift annuity (CGA). Almost every major nonprofit organization offers gift annuities, and they're pretty straightforward and easy to understand. A CGA is a contract between you and a charity in which you give the charity an asset, and the charity gives you a fixed monthly payment for the rest of your life. This way, you keep the income but the charity gets the asset after you die.

This is a good way to transfer cash or assets (usually appreciated assets) to your favorite charity at your death while still giving yourself a guaranteed income stream. An example of this is giving a bank CD to your alma mater. The university pays you a monthly payment for the rest of your life, and the school keeps the CD when you die.

With a CGA, you usually receive a fixed lifetime income stream that's higher than what your asset is currently generating. You can take an income tax deduction, based on IRS tables, that calculates the present value of the future gift. Part of your higher income stream can be tax-exempt. If you transfer an asset that has grown in value, you avoid paying capital gains tax. The asset is removed from your estate, which decreases the overall amount for estate-tax purposes.

Charitable life insurance. With this option, you buy a life insurance policy on yourself and make the charitable organization the beneficiary. This might be a way to maximize your contribution to your favorite charity. You pay the premiums during your lifetime so that your favorite charity receives the often-larger life insurance proceeds at your death. Here's another benefit: if you make the charity the owner and beneficiary of the life insurance contract, you can claim a tax deduction for the ongoing premium payments as you make them.

Charitable remainder trust (CRT). This is another great option, especially if you plan to give larger gifts to charity during your lifetime. Usually, you set up a charitable remainder trust and designate it as the beneficiary of your IRA account.

Doing this gives you a way to donate appreciated property to a charity, such as a stock with a really high taxable gain. At the same time, it allows you to keep the income from the donation. This is because the charitable remainder trust is tax-exempt, similar to a charity.

When you transfer the property to the trust and make the charity the beneficiary, the full appreciated value (cost basis and taxable gain) of the property goes to the trust. That's because the trust doesn't have to pay capital gains tax like you would if you had sold it and written the charity a check for the amount of proceeds. With the charitable remainder trust as the beneficiary of your IRA, the IRA investments go to the trust at the time of your death, and the beneficiary won't have to pay income taxes.

You can designate a charitable remainder trust to provide you with annual payments during your lifetime, even though the charity gets the assets after you die. However, these annual payments are subject to income taxes. This is the opposite of the charitable lead trust we explored earlier.

Here's an example of utilizing a charitable remainder trust: Put your farm acreage that has a long-term lease contract into a charitable remainder trust and make your favorite charity the beneficiary of the trust. Rental income from the lease goes to you each year of your life, but the farmland goes to the charity upon your death.

The downside of a charitable remainder trust is that it's more complicated to set up than other charitable options, and it's irrevocable. Even so, you can exercise some control over the way the assets are invested. You may even switch from one charity to another.

The benefits of a charitable remainder trust are that you can continue to use donated property and/or receive income for the rest of your life. This kind of trust helps you avoid capital gains and estate taxes on donated assets. It also allows you to get an income-tax deduction for the fair market value of the remaining interest the trust earns. I recommend you see an attorney for all of these options, but especially so for a charitable remainder trust.

If you're planning to give part of your estate to charity, it's best to do it strategically so it benefits both you and the charity. One of the most strategic assets to consider donating to charity at death are those in your IRA or retirement plan for which taxes have not been paid. This keeps your beneficiaries from paying estate taxes and federal income taxes on these assets.

Before putting a charitable giving plan into action, discuss it with your financial advisor, accountant, and attorney to see how it may affect your financial and tax situation. The professionals in your life are there to help you find the best option for your situation – one that maximizes your giving while minimizing your tax liabilities.

LETTER TO YOUR BENEFICIARIES

Let's face it: you're going to die sometime, and you can't take anything with you. You may pass away suddenly, due to an unexpected injury or illness, and someone else will get your possessions. The last thing you or your family members want is a fight over the assets you worked your entire life to build. I've heard all kinds of horror stories about families that fight after the death of a loved one. Don't become another one of those stories.

For your family's sake, plan for what becomes of your estate after you die and clearly communicate those plans to your family and other beneficiaries. A detailed letter is a great way to prevent your family from fighting over material possessions.

A letter of instruction doesn't carry the legal weight of a will or trust, but it can make your wishes clear to your loved ones. After someone dies, emotions often run high, and sorting out someone's estate can be complicated. Your letter could help your family and friends navigate this difficult time.

There are a few specifics you may want to address in your letter of instruction. These include:

- A list of your financial accounts, along with account numbers, online user names, and passwords.
- A list of key documents and where to find them. For example: your will, insurance policies, tax returns, bank and investment statements, titles (vehicles, boats, and recreational vehicles), real estate deeds, mortgage information, Social Security and Medicare cards, birth certificate, and marriage and/or divorce papers.
- The contact information for the professionals you use, such as financial advisor, attorney, insurance agent, and accountant.

In this letter, include your wishes for cremation or burial, what you want to happen at your funeral (Scripture, songs, pallbearers, etc.), organ donation, and information that might be helpful in writing an obituary. It's a nice touch to express personal thoughts, memories, or life lessons you want your family and friends to know. Finally, make sure your letter of instruction is in a safe place where your family and friends can find it.

KEY TAKEAWAYS

Regardless of the estate planning tools you use, make an estate plan and put it in a safe place. In addition, frequently review your retirement plan and your estate plan. I suggest you review it annually because tax laws continue to change. A good plan today may not work as well in the future.

Estate planning is important to you and your beneficiaries.

Estate planning is not just for wealthy retirees. Everyone needs a plan – and that includes you. A good estate plan specifies how your property and other possessions are distributed with as few taxes being paid as possible. As you set up your financial plan for retirement, speak with an attorney who can guide you through the process.

Designate someone to make financial and/or healthcare decisions for you.

Choose someone who may speak for you if you're not able to speak for yourself. Powers of attorney and living wills are documents that allow you to legally designate another person to make financial and/or healthcare decisions for you.

Review the legal tools that help you distribute your assets.

Few people die without leaving at least some assets behind: a home, investments, a savings account, etc. A will and/or trust are helpful tools that enable you to distribute your assets to your beneficiaries or heirs. It's important to keep them up-to-date and in a location known to family members and/or legal representatives.

Be strategic in your charitable giving.

If you're planning to give part of your estate to charity, do it strategically so it benefits both you and the charity. There are several methods to use, so I suggest you discuss them with your financial advisor, accountant, and attorney to see how the different options affect your financial and tax situation. Then, communicate and explain your decision to your children in a family meeting, or in your will.

A letter to your beneficiaries helps reduce confusion and conflict.

By spelling out your wishes in a letter, you may save your loved ones some tough decisions – and perhaps even a nasty fight – once you've passed. Plan for the day after your last day on earth.

QUESTIONS FOR PERSONAL OR GROUP STUDY

1. Did your parents engage in estate planning? If so, what did that look like? Was it helpful to you and your siblings?
2. What are the qualities you seek in designating a person to make financial and/or healthcare decisions for you if you're not able to make them yourself? Who comes to mind? Why?
3. What tools are in place to distribute your assets after your death? Which tools were discussed in this chapter that were new to you? Which ones prompt you to take a closer look?
4. Have you considered giving part of your estate to your church or other favorite charity? With which leaders in these organizations should you visit?
5. What would you most want to communicate to your family in a letter that's opened after your death?

CHAPTER SEVEN
FINANCIAL PLAN

"I HAD THE BEST NIGHT'S SLEEP I'VE HAD IN A LONG TIME."

That's what I heard immediately after I answered the phone. "Seriously, I slept so well last night," the caller continued. What made this call so awkward was that it wasn't my wife or another family member on the line. It was a lady who had become a new client the day before this call.

"That's great, so happy for you," I said self-consciously.

She laughed and went on to say that she'd been having trouble sleeping due to anxiety about her upcoming retirement. She said she had felt as if she were driving full speed toward a cliff with no idea what to do about it.

I had met the caller and her husband a few weeks earlier, then gathered information and developed a plan that would enable them to retire and maintain their current lifestyle. I ended my presentation with, "Congratulations, you can retire."

The awkward phone call resulted from my client sleeping soundly because she had made peace with the future.

A successful retirement doesn't just happen. It begins with a good financial plan. In this chapter, I hope to convince you that strategic planning is the necessary first step to a successful retirement.

Let's consider these four key elements of a financial plan:

- Why it's important to write out your retirement plan
- How hiring a professional to help build this plan actually saves you money
- How to get started on a financial plan that addresses your goals
- How to notice the most helpful parts of a financial plan

WRITE OUT YOUR RETIREMENT PLAN

How many times have you wrestled with an important, or expensive, issue and thought, "I'm going to need to see that in writing"? That's because seeing the details helps us evaluate the pros and cons so we make a wise decision.

Benjamin Disraeli, former prime minister of the United Kingdom, wisely said, "The fool wonders, the wise man asks."

Your retirement is too big and too important to merely wonder about. Writing down your retirement plan is the first step to success. Creating a financial plan helps you develop strategies that address a wide range of retirement scenarios. As I wrote at the beginning of this chapter, a successful retirement doesn't just happen. It is thought out, planned out, and put into action.

The process of drafting a financial plan helps more than you may think. It enables you to make some decisions you didn't even anticipate. It allows you to compare strategies side-by-side to see which one works best for you. And it enables you to explore hypothetical income- and spending-plan projections in advance – before circumstances force you into a decision.

> "The fool wonders, the wise man asks."

The sad part is that many people don't plan. The Employment Benefit Research Institute found that sixty-one percent of workers have not thought about how much money they need to withdraw from their retirement savings once they stop working.[1]

Early planning empowers you to maneuver your retirement so you can meet your goals. You have planned out, and maybe even over-analyzed, other major transitions in your life such as buying a home, starting a family, or changing jobs. So, why wouldn't you make a plan for the best part of your life?

The retirement you've been dreaming about deserves a thoughtful plan. That way, you're neither surprised nor disappointed. You need to create a financial plan. I assure you, you'll be thankful that you did.

HIRE A PROFESSIONAL

You could have built your own house. You know a little about foundations and framing. You probably could have subbed out the parts of the house you couldn't safely build yourself. But you didn't, of course, because you knew that hiring a professional builder would save you time and money on something as important as the place your spouse and children sleep.

Your retirement is just as important as your house – maybe more important, because you can always sell a house, or build a new one, but you're stuck with your retirement. Hiring a professional to help you build a financial plan saves you time, and it could potentially save you lots of money by avoiding costly mistakes.

I've always been impressed with the Panama Canal, not just the wonder of how it was built, but the difficulty of guiding a ship through it. The canal averages five hundred feet in width, while the average ship passing through is 106 feet wide. So, ships designed to operate on the open seas, with miles of space on either side, have a margin of error of less than two hundred feet while navigating the canal.

> "You can always sell a house, or build a new one, but you're stuck with your retirement."

The risk of calamity is so great, and the level of difficulty is so high, the operators of the Panama Canal require every ship captain passing through to relinquish full authority to a captain employed by the canal. Once the ship emerges safely on the other side, the ship's captain regains full authority.

Good financial planners – or, we might call them wealth advisors – are like Panama Canal captains. They guide you through the part of your journey that is most difficult and dangerous. The financial plan, which includes implementation, is the tough part. There's little margin for error.

And once you stop working, there's little opportunity to repair a damaged nest egg.

Of course, there's no guarantee that hiring a financial professional makes your retirement problem-free, but it does increase the odds of a financially secure retirement. An experienced wealth advisor helps you think through your financial goals and develop strategies that meet your long-term needs.

There are many financial/wealth advisors. So, do some homework, starting online with brokercheck.finra.org. Make sure the advisor you choose is licensed and has a *designation*, such as Accredited Investment Fiduciary. Avoid the trend of hiring an unlicensed person, such as the agent who handles your home and auto insurance; he or she may try to "sell" you investment products.

Three Financial Industry Regulatory Authority (FINRA) securities licenses are respectable: Series 6, 7, and 66 exams.

The FINRA securities licenses designated **Series 6** mean an advisor has passed an exam and can assist you with certain types of mutual funds, municipal fund securities, variable life insurance, variable annuities, and unit investment trusts. This isn't the highest available license, but it's better than no license at all.

The FINRA **Series 7** securities-licensed person can trade a wide range of investments, such as stocks, mutual funds, options, municipal securities, and variable contracts. Series 7 licenses give a financial advisor considerably more tools to assist you than Series 6 licenses. All American stockbrokers must have a Series 7 license to trade.

An advisor who wants a FINRA securities license **Series 66** must first have a Series 7 as a prerequisite. Advisors who possess both the Series 7 and Series 66, like I do, may also be hired to manage an investment account. Hiring a wealth advisor to buy and sell investments on your behalf gives that person the ability to adapt quickly to changing market conditions without having to ask you first. You establish parameters – for example, how much risk you're willing to take – and the advisor manages your investments and reports back to you periodically.

Financial professionals may obtain many *designations* to indicate they continually improve their knowledge of the financial industry. There are many opinions as to which designations are best, but none of them holds a candle to an advisor's FINRA licenses described above.

I believe the top three credentials to accompany a securities license are:

Certified Financial Planner (CFP), Chartered Financial Analyst (CFA), and Accredited Investment Fiduciary (AIF).

Advisors with the designation of Certified Financial Planner (CFP) have had "rigorous education, training, and ethical standards, and are committed to serving their clients' best interests today to prepare them for a more secure tomorrow."[2] Advisors with this designation are generally good at building financial plans.

Advisors with the designation of Chartered Financial Analyst (CFA) are financial professionals "primarily involved in activities related to the investment decision-making process – generally portfolio managers and research analysts on both the buy and sell-side."[3] Advisors with this designation are usually good at building investment portfolios. They normally work behind the scenes at investment firms.

Advisors with the designation of Accredited Investment Fiduciary (AIF) have had training and passed an exam concerning fiduciary practices. *Fiduciaries* are trained – and sometimes legally required – to maintain the best interests of their clients so they can offer a higher level of trust to those who work with them.

The Accredited Investment Fiduciary designation "is to assure that those responsible for managing or advising on investor assets have a fundamental understanding of the principles of fiduciary duty, the standards of conduct for acting as a fiduciary, and a process for carrying out fiduciary responsibility."[4] Advisors with this designation are good at building trustworthy plans and helping implement them.

Hiring a financial professional adds an experienced perspective to help you achieve your financial goals. Years ago, as a new driver, I remember my dad telling me to never be afraid to pay for good brakes because my life depended on it. In the same way, I advise you not to be afraid to pay for good financial advice when your retirement is at stake.

CREATE A FINANCIAL PLAN

The process for creating a retirement financial plan is much like the planning you do for other significant events in your life. The primary steps are: goal setting; aligning your goals with your finances; implementing your plan; and reviewing/updating.

You begin the process with goal setting as we discussed in Chapter 1. Think through what is most important to you and what is within your reach to create your retirement goal. For example, consider what you want to do, where you'll do it, and who is to accompany you. After you've written down your retirement dreams, see how realistic they are considering the finances you have.

Aligning goals with finances helps put your retirement into focus. With the help of a financial professional, use current spending as a guide to future expenses. Work out a strategy to marry your income potential with your retirement goals.

Next, implement your strategy. Retirement doesn't come with guarantees, but implementing a good financial strategy is a great start toward helping you reach your goals. As the Nike slogan used to say, "Just Do It." Put your plan into action.

Finally, review and update your plan. Once your plan is in motion, you should review it every few years. There are always ups and downs in a retiree's life. One of the greatest reasons for having a financial plan is to help you manage life's uncertainties. A flexible plan that's frequently reviewed enables you to navigate the uncharted waters of advancing age.

As Ayn Rand said wisely, "Money is only a tool. It will take you wherever you wish, but will not replace you as a driver."[5] Creating a retirement plan is an important step in reaching your retirement goals. The process doesn't have to be scary. Simply create a strategy you need for the retirement you want.

> "Money is only a tool. It will take you wherever you wish, but will not replace you as the driver."

A successful retirement isn't a matter of luck. It comes to those who put in the time and effort to be prepared. A good financial plan is a lot like a good GPS map; it helps you get started and keeps you on the right path.

NOTE THE MOST HELPFUL PARTS OF A FINANCIAL PLAN

Your financial advisor may use one or more of the following financial-planning programs: eMoney©, MoneyGuidePro©, or Money Tree©. I have used all of these, but I particularly like Orion Planning©, which I use with my clients. Every advisor has his or her preferences. All of these software packages feature an easy-to-understand format.

Several parts of the financial plan are helpful, such as:

Balance sheet. After your advisor enters your financial information, the planning software creates a professional balance sheet. Seeing your cash and investment holdings in an organized fashion helps you see the makeup of your holdings and your debt. The balance sheet reveals whether your situation is strong or needs attention.

Cash flow report. This report organizes your income sources – such as Social Security, pension, and IRA distribution – and runs them concurrently with your expected living expenses. This gives you a glimpse of retirement from a financial perspective.

When people ask if they can afford to retire, I always start with this report. It shows if you have enough money to last for the rest of your life. It also reveals how much extra cash you may have to pass on to your beneficiaries.

The important point is that you see how things could play out early enough to make adjustments if necessary. I especially like to see the years in which income changes, such as when Social Security begins, business income stops, or when you receive an expected inheritance.

"What if" section. This is where I change the scenarios to see what would happen if you made different choices. Then, you can compare them to the original plan. One scenario is if you took a lump sum from your pension instead of monthly income. Another might include selling your rental properties and investing the difference. Yet another might be waiting until age seventy to begin drawing Social Security rather than starting the benefit earlier.

> **"Your money is going to go three places: to Uncle Sam, savings, or your lifestyle."**

There are several other helpful parts of a financial plan, but the important point is that the plan is customized to your situation. Like my friend Steve Nelson says, "Your money is going to go three places: to Uncle Sam, savings, or your lifestyle." A financial plan helps you determine which of those three gets the most.

KEY TAKEAWAYS

Everyone should have a financial plan.

Early planning enables you to maneuver your retirement so it meets your goals. The retirement you've been dreaming about deserves to be thought out, just like the other major transitions in your life.

Hire a financial professional.

I say this, not because I'm a financial professional, but because it's wise to hire someone anytime you need something done that leaves no room for error. Hiring a financial advisor brings an outside perspective to help you achieve your financial goals. Your advisor may see an opportunity that you never would have considered.

I will never forget the day I told one of my clients he could retire right away, not wait three more years as he had thought. That meeting changed his life. Remember, don't be afraid to pay for good financial advice when your retirement is at stake.

A retirement plan is an important first step.

Creating a retirement plan is a crucial step in reaching your retirement goals. A thorough financial plan helps you make the right investment decisions before you retire. A good financial plan is a lot like a good GPS map; it helps you get started and keeps you on the right path.

A retirement plan helps you set a time to retire.

A financial plan helps you evaluate whether you can retire early. The plan's cash flow report reveals whether you have enough money to last the rest of your life – and it gives you time to make adjustments.

Peace of mind is valuable.

Having a good financial plan gives you peace of mind. It tells you that you've done everything you can to prepare for retirement. I often tell my clients that peace of mind is valuable. You need to make a financial plan. I guarantee you'll be glad you did. Finances should be a comfort, not a worry, as you advance through retirement.

QUESTIONS FOR PERSONAL OR GROUP STUDY

1. Think about major transitions in your life: marriage, career, children, etc. How did you plan for these transitions? And how do those plans encourage you to consider financial planning for retirement?
2. When have you hired professional help? What made you decide it was wiser to seek a pro rather than tackling the project alone? What are some good reasons for hiring a professional financial planner?
3. Did your parents plan well for retirement? What did they do right? Where could they have improved? What can you learn from their experience?
4. What worries you most about retirement? Why? How can a professional financial planner address these worries?

CHAPTER EIGHT
WHERE DO I GO FROM HERE?

"WHICH BASE DO I RUN TO?"

I was coaching first base in a Little League baseball game. Our team had spent a lot of time in practice hitting, fielding, and base running. But I guess I wasn't thorough enough in my coaching. The little slugger just had his first hit. He ran down the base path to first base, bathing in the glow of enthusiastic cheers from the crowd. I gave him a high five and told him to run hard when the next batter hit the ball.

He looked up at me with a helmet two sizes too big and said, "I will run fast, Coach, but which base do I run to?"

I smiled and pointed to second base.

We have discussed everything you need to start preparing for retirement. But before we end this book, I want to point you in the direction you need to go next.

A successful retirement is just around the corner for you. By reading this book, you have already proven you are open to learning more about how to make your retirement successful, and you're ready to take the necessary steps to prepare for it.

In this final chapter, I'm providing practical steps to guide your retirement to success. You might be closer to retirement than the two-year mark where this chapter begins. But don't worry. Just pick up the steps where they apply to your situation.

STEPS TO RETIREMENT

Two years before your expected retirement date, compare your current monthly budget with what you expect your monthly retirement budget to be. Estimate what will change. You might use less fuel in your car since you're no longer commuting to work, and maybe you won't need as many new clothes. Make the budget as realistic as possible, using Chapter 2 of this book as a reference.

Also, look at your retirement health insurance options and decide which one works for your age and family. Look into long-term care and decide whether the need justifies the cost considering your health and family history.

One year from your expected retirement date, meet with a Social Security Administration professional *in person*. Understand the different options available to you and determine when it's best to begin receiving retirement benefits. Take detailed notes and get the contact information of the person you meet with, because sometimes you get different answers from different people.

There are several factors to consider when deciding when to claim Social Security retirement benefits, such as your current age/health, your family's longevity, whether you will continue to work from ages sixty-two to seventy, and whether you have other money available to support you while you bridge the gap until your Full Retirement Age (FRA).

You may need the assistance of a financial advisor to decide which option is best for you. Use Chapter 3 of this book as a reference. Generally, retirees have five healthcare options before they qualify for Medicare:

1. Retirement health insurance continuation from your employer
2. COBRA coverage
3. Public exchanges
4. Private insurance exchanges
5. A spouse's plan

Six months before your expected retirement date, meet with a financial advisor to make a retirement financial plan. The advisor needs to know your retirement goals, the income sources available to you, an estimated retirement budget, and your investment risk tolerance. Set up IRA accounts so you may receive your 401(k) balance when you retire.

Make a list of discussion points for your advisor. For example:

- Where you plan to live, and what your daily and weekly activities will be.
- How your financial situation may change. For example, if your spouse is still working, how long will he or she continue to do so? Also, do you have rental properties or other income sources that could change?
- How your tax situation may change. Are you currently paying estimated quarterly taxes? If so, will this continue?
- When and how you plan to leave your current employer, and how that affects your retirement finances.

Use Chapter 7 of this book as a guide and take the following items to the meeting:

- Your most recent Social Security estimates for you and your spouse
- Your most recent investment statements, including your 401(k)
- Any pension statements that show income options

Review your portfolio annually with your advisor and tell him or her of any significant life changes along the way.

Two months before your expected retirement date, contact your tax preparer to determine what amount of federal and state taxes need to be held out of your retirement investment income, including Social Security. Communicate this information to your financial advisor.

One month before your expected retirement date, make a temporary income plan for the days immediately after you retire. It may take thirty to forty-five days from the date of your retirement to get your 401(k) balance moved and income started.

After you have a retirement plan in place, you can celebrate with a big party and then move into this new and exciting season of life. I remember a high school classmate of mine who couldn't enjoy our graduation party because he didn't know what he was going to do next. Plan well so you can enjoy your retirement party. You don't have to invite your boss to the party if you don't feel like it. This is your special day. Eat a piece of cake for me.

After you retire and have received your final paycheck, contact your employer's human resources department and request transfer paperwork to roll your 401(k) balance into the IRA you previously set up with your financial advisor. (It's best to wait until your final paycheck to make sure you receive all of your employer's 401(k) match.)

When you transfer a 401(k) directly from your company's retirement plan to your IRA, there is no tax consequence. Sometimes, the retirement plan manager mails you the check from the retirement plan. (It's a little nerve-racking to get a check in the mail for a million dollars!) That check is made out to you and the name of the company that set up your IRA. Get that check to your financial advisor as soon as possible. You have sixty days to get it deposited before any taxes are due, but don't mess around with that check. Get it deposited immediately.

Finally, ask your financial advisor to set up your retirement investment income via ACH or check on the fifteenth of every month. You want your income to feel as much like your old paycheck as possible. The first year of retirement can be somewhat scary because of the strangeness of not going to work. Making your income feel like your normal paycheck helps ease some of that anxiety. Use Chapter 5 of this book as a reference.

KEY TAKEAWAYS

Now you know where to go from here.

I hope you've found this book helpful as you prepare for the retirement of your dreams. You needed to ask the right questions to get started. Now, hopefully, you have the answers that enable you to put a plan in place.

"Congratulations, you can retire!"

The best part of my job is showing people their financial plans and telling them they can retire. So let me tell you, you can retire on time and with dignity. You can do this.

Congratulations, you can retire!

QUESTIONS FOR PERSONAL OR GROUP STUDY

1. How close are you to retirement right now? How many steps have you taken toward the financial goals you need to reach?
2. Which step in the retirement-planning process do you dread the

most? Why? What can you do to ease your anxiety about that step?
3. Now that you've read the book, do you feel more confident in knowing how to retire?
4. What still needs to be done to prepare you for retirement?
5. What's the most significant insight you've gained from reading this book?

ADDITIONAL RESOURCES

Retirement Fund Calculators:

www.aarp.org/work/retirement-planning/retirement_calculator

https://money.cnn.com/calculator/retirement/retirement-need/

https://www.calcxml.com/calculators/i-am-retired-how-long-will-my-savings-last?skn=#results

https://www.wiserwomen.org/ (special site for women and retirement)

General Retirement Helps:

https://www.dol.gov/agencies/ebsa/about-ebsa/our-activities/resource-center/publications/retirement-savings-toolkit

> *Savings Fitness … A Guide to Your Money and Your Financial Future*
> *Top 10 Ways to Prepare for Retirement*
> *Women and Retirement Savings*
> *What You Should Know About Your Retirement Plan*
> *Retirement Toolkit*

To order copies, contact EBSA toll-free at 1-866-444-3272.

Social Security Administration:

https://www.ssa.gov/benefits/retirement/

The Social Security website has resources to assist you with making retirement decisions as well.

KEY DEFINITIONS

Annuity – An insurance or investment contract that promises to pay you regular income now or in the future and backed by an insurance company.

Appreciation – When the value of a mutual fund share goes up in value. When the total value of the securities owned by the fund rises, the value of one's fund shares rises with it.

Asset allocation – An investment strategy that has a goal of balancing a person's risk and reward by assigning a portfolio's investments in line with the person's goals, risk tolerance, and timeline.

Bad debt – The type of debt that has no collateral and has frequently been acquired through frivolous or selfish means.

Beneficiary – The person selected to receive the income or ownership of an estate or account from a deceased person.

Budget – A detailed plan of how your financial activity, income, and expenses are expected to go.

Capital gains distributions – When a mutual fund distributes capital gains earned from the fund manager's selling of securities at a profit.

Cash equivalents – Short-term investments, three months or less, that provide safety of principal, are very liquid, but have significantly lower earnings potential than fixed income or equity investing. Examples include: checking accounts, savings accounts, money market funds, short-term CDs, and treasury bills.

Company match – This is the contribution an employer makes for an employee into the employer-sponsored retirement plan. It is usually based on the deferral percentage employees make themselves.

Credit card – A card that enables a person to borrow money or buy things on credit; the balance is paid by the person at a later date.

Defined Contribution Retirement Plan – Known mostly as 401(k) in the for-profit world and as 403(b) in the nonprofit world.

Diversification – The process of spreading out investment funds among a variety of securities so as to minimize risk.

Dividends – When a mutual fund distributes earnings to shareholders that the fund earned from its holdings from stocks, bonds, or other investment income.

Equity – Another name for stock, equities are a type of investment in which the investor actually owns an asset that may increase or decrease in value. Examples include: preferred stock, common stock, real estate, precious metals, and collectibles.

Estate – A person's property in land and other assets and liabilities left by a person after his or her death.

Executor – A person designated as a personal representative to settle another person's estate.

Fiduciary – Anyone who must act in the best interests of his or her client. Fiduciaries are trained, and sometimes legally required, to maintain the best interests of their clients so they can offer a higher level of trust to those who work with them.

Fixed Income – A type of investment in which one loans money to some institution at a specific interest rate and time period. Examples include: certificates of deposit (CDs), fixed annuities, corporate bonds, and government bonds.

Full-time employment – When a person is employed by another for more than thirty hours per week.

Human longevity – The duration of one's life.

Inflation – The continual increase of prices for goods and services over a given time period.

Invest – The attempt to create more money by purchasing shares of companies or financial instruments.

Investment volatility – The erratic rise and fall of investment values due to the unpredictability of the underlying asset in the market.

Liquidity – The concept of easy access to investments for the purpose of converting the investments to cash quickly.

Lump-sum payment – A payment made all at once instead of over time in installments.

Money – Currency, whether in paper, coin, or digital form, that is guaranteed as legal tender by the federal government.

Mutual funds – A type of investment that allows a group of investors to pool their money together to be invested by a professional fund manager to seek a predetermined investment objective.

Nest Egg – A sum of money saved for future use. Another way of saying "retirement account."

Pension fund – A fund set aside by a company to benefit its workers after retirement.

Period certain – An annuity option that guarantees the person's monthly payments will pay out as a minimum, such as for 120 months, in the event that person dies shortly after beginning the annuity payout.

Retire – When a person ceases to work in full-time employment.

Retirement income – The money one earns or receives from savings or pensions, as opposed to the money paid for work produced.

Retirement savings – Money and other financial instruments stored and invested for use during the time the worker is no longer employed in full-time work.

Social Security benefits – Monthly payments from the U.S. government to retired workers or their families who have paid Social Security taxes for at least forty "quarters."

Systematic withdrawal – A payment method of receiving scheduled income (distributions) in regular payments from an investment account.

Volatility (investment) – Describes how often and how severe the stock market fluctuates.

Work – Employment in which one performs acts of labor in exchange for financial compensation.

THE ULTIMATE RETIREMENT

Throughout this book, I offered you guidance about retirement so that you finish well. But I want to go even further, encouraging you to be prepared for what comes after retirement: everlasting life. The Bible tells us we must be saved – that is, have a personal relationship with Jesus – to enjoy everlasting life in heaven and in the new heavens and earth God is preparing for us. If you aren't saved, don't know how to be saved, or don't know if you are saved, then please keep reading.

Consider these questions:

- Who is Jesus to you?
- If you died right now, where would you go? If heaven, why?
- If what you believe were not true, would you want to know it?

If your answer to the last question is "Yes," keep reading.

Read these verses from the Bible and ask yourself, "What does this say to me?"

Romans 3:23 – "For all have sinned and fall short of the glory of God."

I believe this says that every single person has messed up somehow. We have sinned, or made mistakes. None of us is perfect. None of us is like God.

> **Romans 6:23** – "For the wages of sin is death, but the gift of God is eternal life in Christ Jesus our Lord."

When I was a boy, I mowed my neighbors' yards, and they paid me a wage. A wage is the payment due for an act or service. To me, this verse says that the payment due for sin is death – not just physical death, but everlasting separation from God in a place the Bible calls hell.

But God offers us a gift of eternal life. A gift is something you don't earn – in fact, you can't earn it. I also know that the Bible describes heaven – where Jesus is – as eternal life.

> **John 3:3** – "I tell you the truth, no one can see the kingdom of God unless he is born again."

This verse says that none of us goes to heaven unless we are *born again* – that is, unless we have new life in Jesus as we trust in him.

> **John 14:6** – "I am the way and the truth and the life. No one comes to the Father except through me."

In this verse, Jesus says that none of us can get to heaven (because we are all sinners) unless we trust in him and allow his goodness and righteousness to wipe away our sins.

> **Romans 10:9-11** – "That if you confess with your mouth, 'Jesus is Lord,' and believe in your heart that God raised Him from the dead, you will be saved. For it is with your heart that you believe and are justified, and it is with your mouth that you confess and are saved. As the Scripture says, 'Anyone who trusts in Him will never be put to shame.'"

This is awesome! It tells me how to be saved. If a person says with his or her mouth that "Jesus is Lord" (the eternal Son of God who is above all and in charge) and truly believes in his or her heart that Jesus really did come to earth, die on the cross, and rise from the dead three days later, then anyone (that includes all people from everywhere, even the worst sinners) will be saved. Not "might be" saved; *will be* saved.

Believers in Jesus are saved by faith in him. Jesus prepares a place for them in heaven. Their names are written in the Book of Life. And Jesus promises to take them to heaven when they die and bring them back to a restored earth with him one day.

When saved people stand before God, and he says we are sinners deserving death, Jesus our Savior will stand and say, "Their punishment of death has already been served; I died on their behalf."

> **Revelation 3:20** – "Here I am! I stand at the door and knock. If anyone hears my voice and opens the door, I will come in and eat with Him, and He with me."

I believe this means the Lord is tugging on the heartstrings of people, telling them they need to be saved. He's knocking at the door of their hearts, and if they open the door to him, he will save them.

Does this make sense to you? Do you need to be saved? You can know Jesus right now, wherever you are as you read these words. Trust in Jesus. Pray something like this:

"Dear God, I have sinned against you and messed up a lot. I want forgiveness for all my sins. I believe that Jesus died on the cross for me and came back to life again. So, I give you my life to do with as you wish. I want Jesus Christ to come into my life, cleanse me of sin, and make me a new person. I commit to following Jesus from this day forward, and trust him to stay with me every moment until he calls me home to heaven. I ask this not in my own good name, but in Jesus' name. AMEN."

If you sincerely prayed this prayer, please tell a pastor where you live, so he can show you what the Bible says you should do next. If you have questions or do not know a local pastor with whom you may speak, call 1-888-JESUS20 (1-888-537-8720) to speak with someone at the Southern Baptist Convention who is prepared to help you take the next steps of faith.

Running with the call (Hab. 2:2),
Richard

ENDNOTES

INTRODUCTION

1. Alan Gotthardt, *The Eternity Portfolio* (Wheaton, IL: Tyndale House Publishers, 2003), 76.

CHAPTER 1

1. Sources: CDC National Center for Health Statistics, 2018; Social Security Administration, 2018; Society of Actuaries, 2018.
2. U.S. Inflation Calculator, https://www.financialarchitectsllc.com/resources, accessed Aug. 23, 2021.
3. https://www.usinflationcalculator.com/inflation/historical-inflation-rates/, accessed Sept. 17, 2020.
4. Larry Burkett, *Preparing for Retirement: Financial Security in Uncertain Times* (Chicago: Moody Press, 1992), 34.

CHAPTER 2

1. U.S. Inflation Calculator, https://www.usinflationcalculator.com/inflation/historical-inflation-rates/, accessed Nov. 12, 2020.

CHAPTER 3

1. Social Security Administration, "Organizational History," https://www.ssa.gov/history/orghist.html, accessed Nov. 19, 2020.
2. *Ibid.*
3. Social Security Administration, "Learn About Retirement Benefits," https://www.ssa.gov/benefits/retirement/learn.html, accessed Nov. 23, 2020.
4. Social Security Fact Sheet, https://www.ssa.gov/news/press/factsheets/colafacts2021.pdf, accessed Nov. 17, 2020.
5. Social Security Administration, "Workers with Maximum-Taxable Earnings," https://www.ssa.gov/oact/cola/examplemax.html, accessed Dec. 2, 2020.
6. Eligibility, "Social Security Benefits," https://eligibility.com/social-security, accessed Dec. 11, 2020.
7. Social Security Administration, "Social Security Retirement Benefit Claiming-Age Combinations Available to Married Couples," https://www.ssa.gov/policy/docs/rsnotes/rsn2017-01.html, accessed Dec. 3, 2020.
8. J. P. Morgan, "Maximizing Social Security Benefits," https://am.jpmorgan.com/us/en/asset-management/adv/insights/retirement-insights/principles/, accessed Dec. 10, 2020.
9. *US News & World Report*, "Social Security Changes Coming in 2021," http://a.msn.com/00/en-us/BB19ZpJ3?ocid=st, accessed Dec. 14, 2020.
10. Social Security Administration, "Exempt Amounts Under The Earnings Test," https://www.ssa.gov/OACT/COLA/rtea.html, accessed Dec. 14, 2020.
11. Social Security Administration, "Cost-of-Living Adjustment (COLA) Information for 2021," https://www.ssa.gov/news/cola, accessed Dec. 15, 2020.
12. Social Security Administration, "2020 Retirement Benefits," https://www.ssa.gov/pubs/EN-05-10035.pdf, accessed Dec. 2, 2020.
13. *Ibid.*

14. Alicia H. Munnell, MarketWatch, "Social Security actuaries update projections for COVID-19," https://www.msn.com/en-us/money/news/social-security-actuaries-update-projections-for-covid-19/ar-BB1bK3Pf?ocid=uxbndlbing, accessed Dec. 17, 2020.

CHAPTER 4

1. https://kellyepperson.com/show-me-the-money-movie-quotes/, accessed March 10, 2021.
2. https://www.investopedia.com/terms/r/rule72t.asp.
3. William P. Bengen, "Determining Withdrawal Rates Using Historical Data," *Journal of Financial Planning*, Oct. 1994, 173, https://www.retailinvestor.org/pdf/Bengen1.pdf.
4. https://www.forbes.com/sites/wadepfau/2018/01/10/william-bengens-safemax-updated-to-2018, accessed March 30, 2021.
5. Bengen, 179.
6. https://www.blackrock.com/us/financial-professionals, accessed Aug. 11, 2021.

CHAPTER 5

1. Richard Baker, *Biblical Retirement: Preparing for a Christian's Retirement* (Springfield, MO: Finance His Way, 2015), 110.
2. https://www.thebalance.com/how-sequence-risk-affects-your-retirement-money-2388672, accessed Feb. 23, 2021.
3. https://www.investopedia.com/terms/a/assetallocation.asp, accessed Feb. 23, 2021.
4. https://www.investor.gov/additional-resources/general-resources/publications-research/info-sheets/beginners-guide-asset, accessed Feb. 23, 2021.
5. https://personal.vanguard.com/us/funds/tools/stylebox, accessed Feb. 23, 2021.

CHAPTER 6

1. https://www.lawyers.com/legal-info/trusts-estates/how-much-do-lawyers-charge-to-help-with-probate.html, accessed May 6, 2021.
2. https://www.irs.gov/businesses/small-businesses-self-employed/estate-tax, accessed May 7, 2021.
3. https://smartasset.com/taxes/all-about-the-estate-tax, accessed May 7, 2021.
4. https://www.americanbar.org/groups/real_property_trust_estate/resources/estate_planning/power_of_attorney/, accessed May 7, 2021.

CHAPTER 7

1. "Retirement Security: Building a Better Future," https://www.ebri.org/retirement/content/retirement-security-building-a-better-future, accessed June 1, 2021.
2. "Certified Financial Planner (CFP)," https://www.cfp.net/, accessed June 7, 2021.
3. "Chartered Financial Analyst (CFA)," https://www.cfainstitute.org/en/about/vision, accessed June 7, 2021.
4. "Accredited Investment Fiduciary® (AIF®)," https://www.fi360.com/, accessed June 7, 2021.
5. From Ayn Rand, *Atlas Shrugged* (New York: Penguin Group, 1992), 387, https://famguardian.org/Subjects/MoneyBanking/Money/AynRandOnMoney.htm, accessed June 7, 2021.

ABOUT THE AUTHOR

Born to a welder and factory worker, Richard Baker had the good fortune to grow up in the small town of Galena, Missouri. Baker left his hometown after high school and pursued his bachelor's degree at College of the Ozarks, a work college, in Point Lookout, Missouri, where he met and married the beautiful brown-eyed Sara Vaughn.

Baker began his career in finance during his senior year. He obtained his first financial license while still living in his college dorm room. A national bank soon hired him, and within four weeks, he advanced through three positions, promotions he attributed – then and now – to the Lord's favor. By the age of twenty-three, Baker became a regional executive over four financial institutions.

Baker earned a B.S. degree in Business from College of the Ozarks. Later, he added master's and doctorate degrees from Midwestern Baptist Theological Seminary. He has passed the FINRA Series 7, 63, and 66 securities exams and also holds the designation for Accredited Investment Fiduciary.

Baker's business acumen has bolstered his career as an author and speaker. In 2015, he published *Biblical Retirement* and frequently speaks on financial topics from a biblical worldview. This is his second book.

Baker has used his diverse background and expertise to serve as a wealth advisor in Springfield, Missouri, for many years. He's always had a passion for working directly with clients and creating individualized portfolios that are tailored toward their specific needs. He focuses on matching investment and financial-planning strategies to his clients' specific goals and then advises them on asset-allocation decisions, portfolio design, and investment implementation.

His practice has been built helping retirees, business owners, and executives navigate through various financial situations such as retirement planning, business succession, and charitable giving. Additionally, he has implemented strategies to help protect wealth, reduce taxes, and increase family wealth.

Baker was instrumental in establishing several education ministries, including The Bridge Nixa, Springfield Dream Center (a Springfield zone 1 inner-city mission), and Alongside Education Ministries. He has served as a board member of Midwestern Baptist Theological Seminary, Alongside Education Ministries, and was formerly appointed by the North American Mission Board.

In his free time, Baker enjoys teaching pastor schools around the world and has been involved in more than forty international mission trips. He also uses his strategic talents to assist struggling churches. Most notably, he helped a 120-year-old church that was about close its doors. In twenty-one months, he led the church to relocate; negotiated and sold their current building; and negotiated and purchased their new property. He reorganized the leadership, hired new staff, designed and supervised the construction of the new building, and transitioned their former property into an inner-city mission called the Springfield Dream Center – all while running his wealth management practice during the day.

Baker and his wife, Sara, live in Springfield, Missouri, with their daughter, Anna Grace, and son, Micah. Their daughter, Alexandra, and her husband, Domingo, along with grandson, Lieder, live in Nicaragua.

www.ingramcontent.com/pod-product-compliance
Lightning Source LLC
Chambersburg PA
CBHW072059110526
44590CB00018B/3234